AFRICAN ETHNOGRAPHIC STUDIES
OF THE 20TH CENTURY

Volume 23

MARRIAGE AND FAMILY AMONG THE YAKÖ IN SOUTH-EASTERN NIGERIA

MARRIAGE AND FAMILY AMONG THE YAKÖ IN SOUTH-EASTERN NIGERIA

Edited by
DARYLL FORDE

Routledge
Taylor & Francis Group

LONDON AND NEW YORK

First published in 1951 by Percy Lund Humphries & Co Ltd for the International African Institute.

This edition first published in 2018
by Routledge
2 Park Square, Milton Park, Abingdon, Oxon OX14 4RN

and by Routledge
711 Third Avenue, New York, NY 10017

Routledge is an imprint of the Taylor & Francis Group, an informa business

British Library Cataloguing in Publication Data
A catalogue record for this book is available from the British Library

ISBN: 978-0-8153-8713-8 (Set)
ISBN: 978-0-429-48813-9 (Set) (ebk)
ISBN: 978-1-138-58810-3 (Volume 23) (hbk)
ISBN: 978-1-138-58830-1 (Volume 23) (pbk)
ISBN: 978-0-429-49244-0 (Volume 23) (ebk)

Publisher's Note
The publisher has gone to great lengths to ensure the quality of this reprint but points out that some imperfections in the original copies may be apparent.

Disclaimer
The publisher has made every effort to trace copyright holders and would welcome correspondence from those they have been unable to trace.

Procession for the Clitoridectomy Rite of a pregnant bride. See p. 25

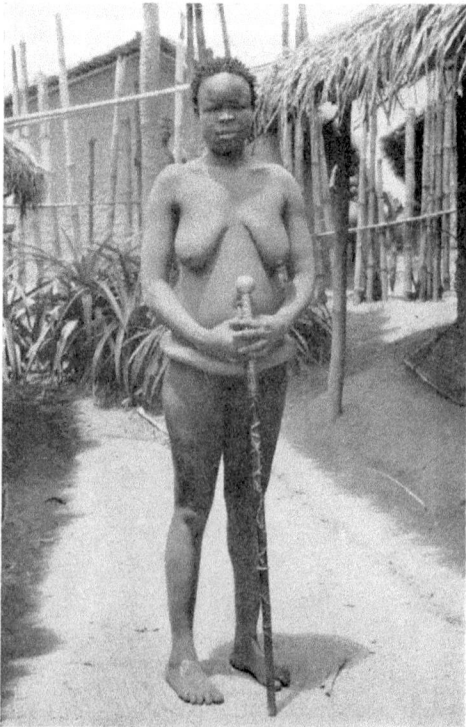

A bride in seclusion after the marriage rites. See p. 36

A youth bringing to his prospective father-in-law a betrothal bundle of creeper rope for yam tying. See p. 16

MARRIAGE AND THE FAMILY
AMONG THE YAKÖ
IN SOUTH-EASTERN NIGERIA

by

DARYLL FORDE, Ph.D.

Professor of Anthropology in the University of London
Director International African Institute

SECOND EDITION

Published for

THE INTERNATIONAL AFRICAN INSTITUTE

by

PERCY LUND HUMPHRIES & CO LTD

12 Bedford Square, London W C 1

1951

PRINTED BY THE REPLIKA PROCESS
IN GREAT BRITAIN BY
LUND HUMPHRIES
LONDON · BRADFORD

To

A. L. KROEBER   and   R. H. LOWIE

in grateful recollection

of

a trans-Atlantic novitiate

This study was first published in 1941 as No. 5 of the London School of Economics and Political Science series of Monographs on Social Anthropology.

With the permission of the London School of Economics this second edition is published by the International African Institute.

C O N T E N T S

List of Illustrations

List of Tables

List of Tables (Contd.)

I INTRODUCTION

This study of Yakö marriage and domestic relations has aimed primarily at analysis of the social values and institutions involved in the establishment and maintenance of marital relationships. This has implied consideration not merely of the conventions through which marital values are expressed but also of the relation of marital status to the general structure of Yakö society. I have also been concerned to determine the extent to which the values posited by the Yakö themselves are actually operative and to discover the changing conditions which have in the period available for study, namely the past two or three generations, been tending to modify traditional standards of marital behaviour. Such conditions will be found to include both circumstances inherent in the social structure and also external factors impinging on Yakö society. I am aware that, apart from technical limitations dependent on the character of the material obtained, the analysis presented here is far from complete, but an attempt has been made to indicate the essential characteristics of Yakö marital standards and practices and the significance of the variations and anomalies observed.

Problems of the relation of personality or temperamental factors to sexual behaviour or to the marital relations between spouses have not, as such, been considered. My experience and data were not adequate for thorough investigation of these matters which, although it would presuppose grasp of the relevant social structure and standardised behaviour patterns is itself psychological not sociological in character.

My work among the Yakö was undertaken in two spells one of six months in 1935 and another of three months in 1939. Particular attention was given to marriage and domestic relations during the second visit. Although the results then obtained did not invalidate the general notions I had formed during the first period of field work they involved some modifications of detail. Prior to this second visit I had referred briefly to marriage in papers published in 1938 and 1939. Where, as occasionally happens, there is some discrepancy of detail between the account given here and the earlier statements this account may be accepted as the more accurate.

I am indebted to the Leverhulme Trustees and their Research Fellowships Committee for the award of a Fellowship and also to the Council of the University College of Wales for leave of absence in order to carry out the field work on which this study is based. My thanks are also due to the Nigerian Government for permission to prosecute these studies and for facilities in the field.

The greater part of my time was spent in Umor, the largest of the five Yakö villages and most of the data are derived therefrom. I was, however, able to assure myself during visits to the other villages and from statements of men and women from these villages who were resident in Umor, that marital conditions were essentially similar throughout the Yako communities. A few minor variations in customary standards and actual practice of sociological significance are considered at the appropriate points in the discussion.

The procedures adopted in pursuing enquiries will be apparent from the exposition itself, but one essential point of method should be emphasised here. In order to determine the actual behaviour involved in marriage and the relation of such behaviour to native ideals it is obviously essential to obtain detailed accounts of particular marital histories. A few such accounts derived from chance encounters, however exhaustive, are likely to be inadequate particularly for determining the degree of variation in respect of particular elements of behaviour. It is therefore desirable to obtain an outline of the marital histories of all the members of a considerable group which can be regarded as a representative sample, and likely to include within itself all the types of situation occurring in the community as a whole. For the Yako such a group was at hand in the households of the men of one patrilineal clan which had been selected at random, and ascertained to be in no marked degree exceptional, during my earlier period of work in 1935, when I was concentrating attention on the social organisation and economy of the Yako. In 1939, with the co-operation of the people themselves, I obtained marital histories of the men and women of all these households and investigated more fully those which appeared to be distinctive in respect of any particular aspect. In this way records for over a hundred men and over two hundred women of all ages were obtained. By means of the age set system a chronological classification of marital practices among these people could be carried out and this has made it possible to determine the period and rate of certain changes during the past fifty years. The number of cases has also been sufficient to apply some simpler statistical methods for the determination of variability in behaviour, including the incidence of polygyny, divorce and other features of Yako marriage. I obtained in addition marital histories of most of the more eminent and well to do men including the priest-heads of the patrilineal and matrilineal clans in order to determine the effects if any on marital practice of social eminence and wealth.

The outlines of the general organisation of Yako society have been indicated in earlier publications and the relevant structural features will be described briefly in the course of this exposition; but the following demographic and economic matters are also necessary for understanding the social context of marriage. The Yako people, one of the several linguistically distinct groups which occupy the territory extending eastward from the Cross River to the mountainous country of the Oban Hills, occupy a continuous tract of country which reaches to the

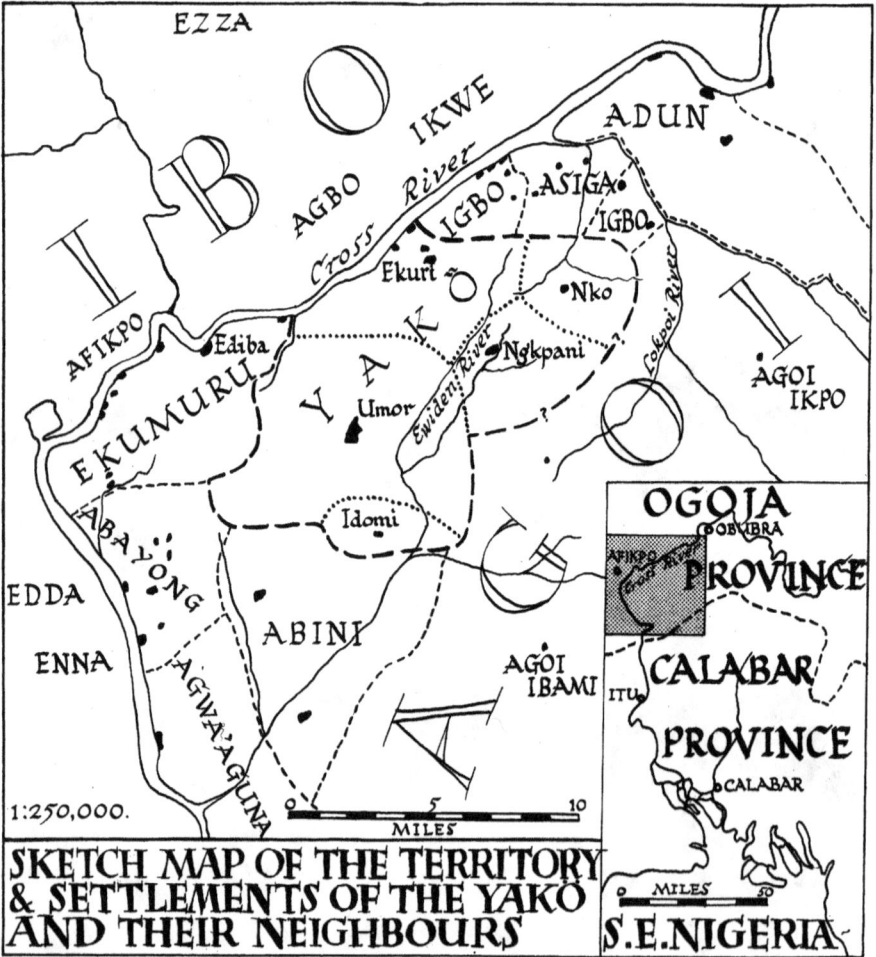

Fig. 1.

river at its north-eastern extremity but is for most part separated from
it by the territories of other linguistic groups,   Ekumuru, Akunakuna,
Abini etc.   Thus the Yakö are not a river trading people and until the
twenties of this century very few of them passed beyond the boundaries
of their own territory or those of their immediate neighbours.   Trading
expeditions to distant centres including the ports for the sale of palm
products or the purchase of stocks of trade goods are a recent development confined to a few younger men.   Yakö women still leave their own
territory very rarely save for daytime visits to riverside village markets (see Map, Fig.1).

The Yakö probably comprise about 20,000 persons in all at the
present time.   They are grouped in five village settlements each situated
from three to six miles from its neighbours. The largest village, Umor,1
seven miles to the east of the river is a large and compact settlement
covering an area of a quarter of a square mile with a population which
I estimated at nearly eleven thousand in 1935.   Six miles to the north
lies Ekuri, somewhat smaller than Umor, of which the main settlement
areas are again away from the river although one of its dispersed wards
has a waterside hamlet.   To the north-east of Umor are the two smaller
and closely neighbouring settlements of Nko and Ngkpani, five and eight
miles away, while little more than three miles south of Umor is the
fifth and smallest village of Idomi. The linguistic unity of the Yakö
corresponds to a very high degree of general cultural homogeneity maintained by a continual flow from one village to another of small numbers
of visitors temporary residents and migrants: But there is no cen-
tralised political organisation. Although a well recognised sense of
their cultural unity exists among the Yakö and there are between some of
the villages traditions of friendship and mutual aid against enemies,
each village has retained a political autonomy commensurate with its
economic self-sufficiency. Sporadic fighting between the villages,
particularly between Umor and Ekuri, has occurred in the past while
inter-village jealousies have been an obstacle to the establishment of
a unitary administrative organisation for local self-government under
British rule. On the other hand an individual Yakö who has a sponsor
and host is readily adopted into the patrilineal clan and territorial
organisation of another village. Ties of matrilineal kinship, unlike
patrilineal, are not abrogated by permanentmigration to another village
and in fact matrilineal kinship relations between persons of different
villages are continually re-created by inter-village marriages in consequence of which a man in one village has sister's sons in another.

1This spelling is not phonetic; the name was variously heard as ume and
umo. This village is commonly known to neighbouring peoples by its
Akunakuna name Ugep and is so named in most Government maps and reports.

4

These in turn lead to further migrations of both men and women from one village to join matrilineal relatives in another. Such migrations are however very few in number in relation to the total populations of the village communities concerned.

By far the greater part of the food supply of the Yakö is obtained from the cultivation of farm plots and most of the labour for each plot is provided by a household unit of which the productive nucleus is a man and his wife or wives. The exploitation of wild oil palms which provide the one substantial surplus of goods saleable for currency in external markets is similarly carried on by household units in which the man collects fruits from palms in the farming area of his patrilineal clan while the wife carries out the greater part of the process of oil extraction and cracks the nuts for kernels. Investigation in 1935 of one patrilineal clan showed that of 112 adult males 105 were heads of households engaged in farming and of the remainder only one was engaged in trading to the exclusion of farming while the others were dependents incapable through age or infirmity of farm work. Half the households in this group were regularly engaged in the production of palm oil and kernels for sale.[1] Thus the maintenance of a farm and, to a lesser extent, of palm oil production are basic activities of the household, and the concern of every husband and wife, while marriage, as will be seen, is the normal means of establishing or extending a household productive unit. There are as will be seen mutual relations of the greatest significance between marriage as a social institution and the conditions of household production.

Note on Orthography: Yakö terms and texts are expressed here in the phonetic system of the International Institute of African Languages and Cultures as set out in 'Practical Orthography of African Languages' (Memorandum 1, 1930) with the following modifications:

(i) the symbol j, not z, has been used for the sound indicated by j in French jeu and by s in English 'pleasure'

(ii) The symbol c is used for the sound indicated by sh in English 'show'

(iii) the velar n as in English 'sing' is represented by ng and if 'hard g', indicated by g, should anywhere follow velar n the combination will be written ngg.

(iv) the several o and u vowels are indicated by diacritical marks thus:

---

[1] See Forde, Land & Labour in a Cross River Village, Geog. Journ.,90, 1937, pp.24-51.

o = open o as in English hot;

o̅ = close o as in English host;

ö = obscure o, or central vowel, approximately as in French jeu but less rounded;

ө = middle o, approximately as in English law.

u = open u, as in English duck

u̅ = close u, as in English pull

(v) Other vowel symbols have their so called Italian values; tones, length and stress have not been indicated.

Earlier Publications on the Yakö

1. Land and Labour in a Cross River Village, Geographical Journal, Vol. 90, 1937.

2. Fission and Accretion in the Patrilineal Clans of a semi-Bantu community in Southern Nigeria, Journal of the Royal Anthropological Institute, Vol.68, 1938

3. Notes on some Population Data from a Southern Nigerian Village, Sociological Review, Vol.30, 1939 (with Dr.E.Charles)

4. Kinship in Umor-Double Unilateral Organisation in a semi-Bantu Society, American Anthropologist, Vol.41, 1939

5. Government in Umor, Africa, Journal of the International Institute of African Languages and Cultures, Vol.12, 1939.

CHAPTER II

II   THE SIGNIFICANCE OF KINSHIP AND AGE SET SYSTEMS

The procedure whereby a Yakö marital relationship is established
or dissolved cannot be understood apart from kinship and age set systems which provide its structural framework. These systems will be
considered here only in so far as they are relevant to the sociological analysis of marriage and the family.

The Yakö kinship system, as has been shown elsewhere, is dual in
character.[1] Patrilineal kinship affords the organising principle of
a system of major territorial descent groups known as yepūn (sing.
kepūn) which will be referred to as patriclans.[2] Each village has an
independent and exclusive patriclan system, and each of the clans
claims collective rights to residential and farming areas in a village
territory. The patriclans are strictly exogamous so that every marriage
involves relations between two distinct sets of patrikin, those of the
groom and those of the bride, and a wife on marriage becomes a member
of the residential group composed of her husband's patriclansmen and
their households. Within a kepūn the sentiment of patrilineal kinship
is more strongly developed between the members of subgroups or lineages known as yeponama (sing. epōnama) whose members trace actual
patrilineal descent from a single ancestor four or five generations
senior to the younger adults. The coherence of the kepūn as a whole
appears to depend as much on the interest in maintaining common residence and farming rights as on the sentiment of patrilineal descent
in terms of which it is expressed. Within a patrilineage however common descent as such is dominant and, in the event of adoption into
another clan, claims of patrikinship may conflict with the formal
relationships proper to clan affiliation.

At the same time a matrilineal kinship reckoning is dominant in
determining the succession to property among the Yakö and ritual values
unify bodies of persons who claim common matrilineal descent and con-

---

[1] Kinship in Umor — Double Unilateral Organisation in a semi-Bantu
Society, Amer.Anthropologist, 41,1939, 523 ff.

[2] The convenient device of using patri-and matri- as prefixes to indicate succinctly the unilineal directions of descent and affiliation
has been suggested and used by W.E. Lawrence in Studies in the Science
of Society, ed. G.P. Murdock, New Haven, 1937. It is adopted here and
applied generally in distinguishing clans, lineages and kinsfolk of
patrilineal and matrilineal affiliation respectively.

stitute matriclans known as yajima (sing. lejima). Here again lineages or kejimafat (sing. lejimafat) of matrikinsmen who trace actual common matrilineal descent are united by stronger sentiments of kinship as distinct from common interests in particular ritual values and symbols. The lejima is not strictly exogamous at the present time and no specific penalty for infringement operates to maintain matriclan exogamy but intra-clan marriages are generally held to be dangerous and conducive to sterility or the early death of children. In fact they very rarely occur.

Although the principle of patrikinship determines the formation and maintenance of primary settlement units in a Yakö village community the grouping of these units in larger divisions or wards of the village known as yekpatŭ (sing. kekpatŭ) ignores this principle and is determined by territorial proximity alone. In the largest village, Umor, there are twenty two patriclans grouped in four wards, but the clans of any one ward are not conceived as segments of a higher ward kin group. The traditions of the clans and genealogical evidence of recent fissions of clans and migrations of one segment to another ward also contradict any such notion.[1]

The ward (kekpatŭ, pl. yekpatŭ) is a territorial group whose coherence derives from the common interests of the men of the co-resident patriclans. A number of economic, ritual and administrative activities are organised within each ward which also has its independent age set system. A new age set or ekō (pl. nkō) of men is formally recognised every three or four years at a feast provided by the new set for the benefit of all the existing sets. The new set consists of the young men who have married or reached marriageable age since the previous set was established. It is called into existence by the ward head to whom it declares its two chosen leaders. Four years is regarded as the proper interval between the formation of two sets and in the past this interval appears to have been generally observed; but in recent years, with increasing population, the interval between calling for the leaders of one set and the next has tended to fall. In Umor three year intervals appear to have occurred recently in Ukpakapi ward while one interval of only two years was recorded for the larger ward of Idjūm. At the same time the ceremonial recognition of an age set has sometimes been postponed for several years on account of failure by the new set to accumulate in good time the food supplies necessary for the feast. Thus the Ukpakapi set whose leaders were called for by the ward head and recognised in 1936 did not give their establishment feast until 1938.

---

[1] See Forde, Fission and Accretion in the Patrilineal Clans of a Semi-Bantu community in Southern Nigeria, Journ. Royal Anth. Inst., 68, 1938, 311 ff.

8

At any one time there are 17 or 18 sets in existence in each ward and among them are distributed men ranging in age from seventeen or eighteen to over seventy years, but the numerical strength of the sets diminishes sharply after middle age with increasing seniority. In the wards of Umor in recent years an age set of men has been of the order of thirty or more strong at the time of formation. The age sets in each ward are alternately labelled okprike and agbiagban, terms for which no convincing etymology was obtained, and each set is further identified by the name of its senior leader,being known as the okprike or agbiagban of so and· so.

The sets of the different ward, although they are formed independently and there is no co-ordination of establishment ceremonies, are in practice equated. Thus a man of one ward in a village can name the sets which correspond with his own, and are regarded as equivalent in age, in the other wards. In the same way, although it is less frequently needed, a man in one village can determine the age set of any ward in another village which is held to correspond in seniority with his own. Should he migrate when adult he will be regarded as a member of such a set in the ward of his new residence. Owing to more frequent reductions of intervals between age set formations in the large Idjūm ward of Umor two groups of two sets are equated with two single sets in the other three wards.

This age set system affords a means of determining the approximate chronological age of any person of which use will be made later in investigating trends in marital customs. The assumption of a four year interval between sets corresponds very well with the age obtained independently for particular men by means of dated events at their births[1] and first marriages. In referring to the successive age sets

---

[1] Thus for example an Ukpakapi man of age set.V, the approximate age of whose members is estimated to be 62-65 in 1939 was independently estimated from occurrence of his first marriage in the year of a British military expedition through the Cross River country to be 61 years old. In the same way, a man of age set XVI. (the age of whose members is estimated at 22-25 in 1939) could be shown to be 26 years of age since the year in which he went away to school was 1925 and that was also the year of the second time that his father who farmed a six year cycle of plots had again cleared a farm on the particular land (Ebe) where he was farming when his son was born. The man was thus 12 years old in 1925 and 26 years in 1939. Similar independent age estimates have confirmed the estimates of the age ranges of other sets.

in this discussion roman numerals will be used to indicate them in order of juniority. The senior set in Ukpakapi ward in Umor, of which
there were only two or three living members in 1935, is labelled I and
the most junior which was formed in 1938 is indicated as XVIII. Age sets
of other wards have been given corresponding numbers according to the
native equations between sets.

But the principle of age grouping operates long before the formal
recognition of a set and a man's age set membership has in fact been
already established in childhood. Thus every year in Umor on one day
during the village festival of Lebokū the children living in each patriclan area form a number of parties each of about the same age, boys and
girls forming distinct sets of parties. Each visits the homes of its
members' parents to collect materials for a feast. The parties of younger children are told that they must choose a leader; the older already
have a leader or dispute over the leadership and settle the matter with
the encouragement of their elders by wrestling contests between rivals.
The boys' parties of similar age from the various yepūn of a ward compete with one another or in groups during the Lebokū festival and at
other times in wrestling and other games. There are squabbles as to
which parties from the different yepūn are equivalent in age and should
therefore compete or join together in these games and there are also disputes as to the appropriate party to which a particular child should
belong. Thus gradually during their childhood the boys of a ward sort
themselves out into a series of groups of increasing seniority and as
the members of each group reach the age of marriage it is formally established as an age set. If however a potential set is too large or too
few in number in the opinion of the ward head it can be split or joined
to its next junior group at this time.

Age groups are similarly formed among the girls of a kepūn and ward
during childhood and the separate groups are distinguished in the ward
dancing parties which take place especially during and after the Leboku
festival. But women's age sets similarly formed by combinations of the
smaller groups, although they choose leaders and like those of the men
act corporately in performing tasks such as path weeding at the request
of the ward head, are not formally established in a public ceremony like
those of the men.

An age set of men continues to be divided within itself into a number of groups of closer friends or companions known as liboma (sing.
koboma = fingers). Such a group of companions, for which the term age
mates as distinct from age set members will be used, consists of half a
dozen or more men mostly, but not entirely, from a single patriclan.
Particular attention must be paid to the koboma and its count-
erpart among women since the celebration of a marriage is the occasion
for displays of mutual esteem between the spouses and their parents on

the one hand and their respective sets of age mates on the other, while the conduct of the marriage rites and feasts are directed by the koboma of the father of the bride and by the corresponding group of companions of her mother, known as a leteko̎.

The group of age mates is conceived as a subgroup of the larger age set and an analogy with lineages of a clan is made: "We have liboma in eko̅ just as we have yepōnama in kepūn." But the age mate groups are not strictly mutually exclusive and comprehensive subdivisions of an age set. A man may, although it is exceptional, belong to more than one koboma at the same time so that the memberships of the various groups overlap to some extent. Membership of a koboma can be terminated at will by simple refusal to continue to recognise the relationship, but, secession or virtual expulsion as a result of quarrels which would render the koboma unstable is said by Yako̎ to occur very rarely. The composition of a koboma although affected by kepūn and lineage affiliations is not co-extensive with the membership of any one patri-lineage or patri-clan in an age set, and a koboma is not conceived as a kin group. Furthermore even the ward boundaries of the age set system can be overstepped by accepting in an age mate group a man of an equivalent age set in another ward. Thus a man of the lineage of Kikungku̅la kepūn in Idjum ward at Umor had as koboma fellows seven men of his own patriclan, five other men of his ward each from a different patriclans and three men of two different patriclans in another ward. The koboma of a man of Ukpakapi ward included three men of his own patriclan, two of another patriclan in Ukpakapi, one of another ward and one or two others whose clan and ward affiliations were not recorded.

An age set is concerned in any marriage or death of one of its members or of a member's close relatives, and it will be shown later how considerable is the part of the relevant age sets in the conduct of the rites and feasts whereby marital status is established. But the entire age set does not usually function as a corporate group on these occasions, the age mates of the member concerned are the main participants to whom may be added less intimate age set fellows who have other ties with him.

CHAPTER III

PRE-MARITAL RELATIONS AND BETROTHAL

As has been indicated above boys and girls are encouraged from early childhood by their parents and elders particularly during the annual Leboku rites to form small parties of age mates. A group with common kepūn affiliation usually provides the nucleus for each party but membership of a party is not strictly confined to children of one kepūn. The girls groups are the more conspicuous because those of successive ages from about nine to sixteen years in one or more yepūn combine to form large dance parties which during and after the Lebokū rites visit the ward and kepūn squares of the village. Forming a circle of twenty to forty performers arranged in a descending order of age groups they execute a shuffling dance to the accompaniment of a large repertoire of songs. Age mates also join together in daily water carrying parties to fetch water for their parents on the outskirts of the village. During the Lebokū rites mutual declarations of friendship are made by girls of a small party, half a dozen or so in number, who regard themselves as a group of intimate age mates. Such a group will usually consist mainly of members resident in a single patriclan area. Taking the coconuts provided by their parents or later their lovers as Lebokū gifts they meet together. One takes the lead and slicing half through a nut with a matchet calls the name of her closest friend. The friend completes the cut calling the name of another friend who then slices the next nut while calling the name of another girl of the group. This continues until all the names have been called. It is from this ceremony that a group of girl companions receive the name letekö friends. These declarations are usually made publicly in the presence of other ward age groups and there are sometimes quarrels over the admission of particular girls into one of these groups of age mates. Thus the letekö, or small group of intimate friends within a potential age set of women, is established early and is very conspicuous among the girls of a Yakö village, and it forms the setting in which its members establish friendship and sexual relations with youths.

Although girls are expected to give their mothers considerable help in the household and farm from an early age, parents interfere little with the leisure and play of their daughters. Boys and girls do not play or move about together either in pairs or in groups in the village, but a boy can obtain an invitation from a girl to be her partner in night parties of her letekö. From the age of eleven or twelve years a party of girl age-mates not merely dances and passes much leisure time as a group but also spends nights together sleeping in one or other of their mothers' houses. To these night parties known as yeyomö, sing. keyomö, each girl is free to invite a lover and the couples occupy the wide mat covered floor of a Yako woman's house. The mother with her young children may remain in the house occupying the raised bed on one side of the large single room, but she is not regarded as a chaperone and will often go to her husband's house if her daughter's leteko wishes to occupy her own.

A boy seeks an invitation to become the partner of a girl in a night party by offering her a customary gift which is presented to her by one or two of his age mates. The boy may have been acquainted with the girl since early infancy but will not approach her directly. With one or two close age mate friends he goes to a place where he is likely to encounter her and stands a little way off while his friends approach her. The traditional gift is a coconut but today a halfpenny or a penny is usually offered in its stead. His friends say that they bring the coconut from the boy who has admired her when he has seen her in the village. It is customary to convey some particular compliment about her beauty or grace and say that the suitor wishes to join her at her next keyomb. Acceptance of the gift requires the girl to tell the go-betweens when and where the suitor may join her or to send a message to them later by one or two of her friends. If she wishes to refuse the approach a girl usually treats it as a joke or pretends that she does not join any night parties. A girl occasionally invites a youth to join her, but such an approach must be indirect and ambiguous for fear of the ridicule that would follow blunt refusal. There is therefore usually some flirtatious encounter before a girl gives an invitation. She then asks one of her friends to take a message to the youth pretending that he has already approached her. The friend will say "So and so is going to be in such and such a house this night. She would like you to come to her as she has had so many messages from you." If the youth wishes to come he pretends he had indeed made approaches but if averse he may well tell the messenger quite bluntly that he has sent no message and that her friend is shameless. From the instances known to me it appears that while approaches are made in this way to men by young widows or divorcees it is exceptional for an unmarried girl to send a definite message of invitation to a youth.

Girls sleep together in parties with their lovers at irregular intervals, often after they have danced in the evening, but I was not able to estimate the frequency of these parties. Among the younger girls of ten or eleven years it is probably occasional and may begin with the consent of the mothers at the urging of older groups who tell them it is time for them to form a night party. But it was generally agreed among my informants in Umor that most girls join night parties before the age of first menstruation.

Before betrothal a girl is at liberty to accept the approaches of several youths on different occasions. Boys and girls gossip a good deal among themselves over who has secured the favour of a particular girl, and whether so and so is jealous of another. It is expected of a boy that he will bring presents such as coconuts, native 'pears', a pot of pomade or a trinket from time to time if he wishes to retain the affection of a girl.

Although a boy is free to visit more than one girl, so long as the girls belong to different groups of age mates, and a girl may on separate occasions invite different lovers, it is considered improper for a boy to court more than one girl at the same time from a single group of age mates. If a lad has visited a keyomö of one letekö as the lover of one girl he cannot quickly transfer his attentions to another without bringing on himself and the second girl the hostility of the rest of the group which will if necessary ostracise the offending girl. The likelihood of this hostility appears to be a very effective deterrent to rivalry between girls of the same letekö, and if a girl does accept the advances of a youth who has recently been the lover of one of her intimates she will probably be forced to leave the group and attempt to join another. On the other hand a girl who shows too openly her jealousy of a lover's friendship with girls in other groups will be laughed at and teased.

Although youths of a single koboma do not as a group offer themselves as lovers to a single letekö of girls there is a tendency for the boys to keep together so that a youth will seek lovers for his friends in a letekö where he himself has found favour.

Usually the lovers who join a party of girls are boys of their own age but a young married man may also join a party of older girls. These parties are the occasion for much general gossip, joking and teasing. Although sexual attraction for a particular partner underlies the presence of each youth all my informants agreed in giving the impression that a single couple could not isolate itself from the rest of the group, that love making tended to be covert and that coitus could take place only secretly when most of the party had settled down to sleep.

All my older informants were agreed that there had during the past generation been considerable change in pre-marital sexual relations and in the attitude of both parents and young people towards them. It appears that sexual play between boys and girls has always been regarded as both inevitable and desirable, and that the night party is the recognised setting for the first phase of sexual experience. To meet a lover elsewhere on the other hand would be shameful. At the same time the earlier attitude, which many of the older people and especially woman retain, is that pre-marital pregnancy is disgraceful and pregnancy before betrothal still more so. Mothers were formerly successful as a rule in impressing on their daughters both before and during betrothal the shame of pregnancy before marriage, they exhorted them to refuse actual coitus and to tell them if any youth attempted to abuse friendship by trying to force it upon them. Although, as will be seen later,

abortion is regarded as a grave offence against the fertility spirit of
the matriclan and one for which supernatural punishment of the whole
clan is to be feared, mothers not infrequently carried out or connived
at secret abortion if their daughters actually became pregnant before
marriage. To guard against penetration the older girls were expected
to wear a special girdle at night parties consisting of a long narrow
strip of cloth, formerly bark cloth, which was wound round the waist
and between the thighs. Older women insist that in their childhood no
young girl would have dared, before betrothal at least, to remove this
girdle lest her friends or her mother discovered it and shamed her. They
also claimed that it would be quite exceptional for a youth to attempt
actual coitus at a night party. When after betrothal the young couple
were allowed to spend the night together in the house of the girl's
mother coitus did sometimes occur but it was not the rule and was
usually interrupted in an endeavour to avoid pregnancy.

At the present time, as is indicated by the very high incidence of
pregnancy before marriage, coitus generally occurs during betrothal and
my younger informants said it was very general between partners in the
night parties of the older girls. But younger people said that today a
girl would usually refuse coitus unless she wishes to be married to her
lover, and even then would try to avoid insemination by insisting on coitus
interruptus. On the other hand I heard of cases in which girls invited
completed coitus in the hope of pregnancy which would force the hands
of parents who disapproved of the youths they wished to marry.

Before the first marriage of a girl there is usually a considerable
period, which may be termed the period of betrothal, during which the
suitor is recognised by the girl's parents as a prospective son-in-law.
In seeking this recognition the suitor has to present himself formally
to the girl's father,[1] and once gained it involves the suitor in obligations to perform specific services for the bride and her parents and
to present gifts to them, especially at times of festival. These gifts
and services are referred to as kokōla, a term which may be used with
reference to any gift but in this context implies the whole series of
obligations preliminary to the marriage rites.

In presenting himself to the girl's father the suitor relies on the
support of one or two of his age mates. His closest friend may go to

---

[1] I refer to the father throughout but a foster-father may act in this
capacity in some circumstances even when the father proper is still a-
live and in the village. A foster-father is usually a step-father or a
mother's brother. In the latter case his household is usually distinct
from that of the girl and her mother.

the father's compound in advance to say that the suitor will come the
next evening or on the next kokö – the main market day when most people
remain in the village – to offer kokōla to the father. With his age
mates, one of whom carries a calabash of palm wine, the suitor arrives
'to show himself'. He usually says little or nothing himself and one
of the friends acts as spokesman, describing the suitor as a friend of
the girl on whose behalf the suitor is anxious to make betrothal gifts
to her parents. I did not witness one of these visits but gained the
impression from informants that they occurred only after the willing-
ness of the parents to accept the suitor had been ascertained either
by the girl or by one of the suitor's friends or older relatives. Little
directly connected with the prospective marriage is usually said at
this visit; the father will have found out elsewhere whether the suitor
or his relatives are able and likely to make a prompt marriage payment
in due course and he will already have discussed with his wife and
their relatives the eligibility of the suitor. The father alludes to
the betrothal services which are expected and indicates that he will
want to see them carried out. The wine is poured out and drunk by the
group and any friends or relatives of the father who may be present in
the compound, and the suitor departs with his friends. There is no
necessary or formal communication between the suitor's father and his
prospective father-in-law at this time.[1]

After betrothal the suitor is usually free to visit the girl in
her house at night apart from parties of her age mates, and each expects the other to refrain from sexual intimacy with others, an expectation which is by no means always fulfilled. Jealousy often leads to
quarrels, while on the other hand a betrothal that is no longer desir-
ed by one partner is often ended by flagrantly consorting with another
lover.

---

[1] In an earlier reference to Yako marriage (Kinship in Umor, Amer.Anth.,
41,1939,523 ff.) I stated that a father might encourage a man to seek
marriage with his (the father's) sister's daughter, that is with a woman
whose son would, in consequence of the matrilineal inheritance of moveable property, be heir to the father's own heir (his sister's son and
also in such a case the brother of his son's wife). Instances of such
marriage were encountered and succession to property was recognised as
a motive for them. But further enquiry has shown that this form of
cross-cousin marriage is to be regarded as an irregular and not as a
preferred type of marriage. In addition to strict patriclan exogamy and
a less stringently enforced matriclan exogamy cousin marriage in any
form is generally regarded as improper among the Yako. There is no pro-
hibition of or penalty for cousin marriage as such but it is considered
undesirable because "the children of brothers and sisters are sons and
daughters',

The customary services of the suitor to his prospective father-in-law consist in Umor of farm work during the following farming year. December or January, the time between harvest and the beginning of the work on the new farm, is commonly chosen by a lover to 'show himself' to his prospective father-in-law. When the father-in-law is ready to clear his new farm in February the suitor has to provide a working party for bush clearing by mustering a group of his age-set fellows to join him there on an appointed day. This group usually consists of the suitor's age mates together with other men or youths of his age-set and some older friends in his patriclan. Nowadays the group may not be more than a dozen strong and visits the farm only on one day, but old men said that when they were young a suitor had to provide a large party on several days.

The suitor has also to provide his prospective father-in-law with a supply of split creeper stems used in considerable quantity on every farm for lines running between poles on which the yam vines are trained and for tying yams on the yam stack frames after harvest. The suitor again seeks the aid of his age mates and other age set fellows and relatives in collecting this during the bush clearing period and it is then coiled into a large tapering bundle, nearly a foot thick at the base and eight or more feet high - the traditional form in Umor in which the gift should be presented to the father-in-law. The suitor has to provide a meal, actually supplied by his parents, and palm wine for his age-mates and other helpers when they return to the village with him after assisting in performing any of these services. (See Frontispiece.)

Sometimes the suitor with his age mates contributes to the work of house building or repairing in place of, or in addition to, farm services. Providing materials for and making new roof mats, of which several hundred are needed for a Yakö house of average size, were cited in several betrothal histories that I recorded. My impression is that as a group activity replacing farm services this practice is recent but that the father-in-law could always by custom, during the betrothal period, call on the suitor himself to assist in house repairing, a considerable task requiring several pairs of hands which is carried out in the slack period before the main yam harvest. A suitor is, indeed, expected to offer his help in any considerable task that the father-in-law undertakes during the period of betrothal. He will, for instance, help in the lifting and tying of yams at harvest, and it is while rendering such aid that the relations between them become to some degree intimate.

During the annual Leboku rites, at the time when parents give special food and ornaments to their children, a suitor should make gifts not only to his betrothed but also to her parents. Items which recur in my records of Leboku gifts of suitors are palm wine, kola nuts (lebū), fathoms of cloth and matchets to the fathers; kola nuts and sets of chewing sticks, made from etung root which blackens the teeth, to the mothers; and to the girls bowls of native 'pears' (kopeng) the fruits of a cultivated tree (pachylobis edulis) which are in season at the time of the Lebokū rites, coconuts, lengths of raphia fibre for making girdles, and bowls of lidua or alōwa fruits from the seeds of which a black dye (eblömi) for decorative body painting is prepared with charcoal. When groundnuts are ready for harvesting shortly after the Lebokū rites it is the turn of the girl to make a customary gift of a bowl of groundnuts to her future husband. This is brought to him by her closest friend and the youth is expected to place a return gift in the empty bowl when handing it to the friend. At the present time the usual return gift is a 'vanity' trade article such as a comb, mirror or necklace. These groundnuts should have been harvested from a crop planted by the girl herself. At the beginning of the farming season after a suitor has presented himself to her father a betrothed girl is given a small patch in her mother's section of the farm which she cultivates and plants with groundnuts for this purpose.

There are differences in the customary obligations of betrothal between the different Yakö villages. I did not investigate these systematically but the following practices in Ngkpani which are not found in Umor will serve to illustrate the character of the variations. At Ngkpani when a girl is betrothed she and her age mates, most if not all of whom will also be betrothed, must refrain from eating keplö (i.e. mashed yam generally known by the pidgin term 'fufu' in Southern Nigeria) during the period from the opening of the farming year after her betrothal until the second following harvest time which should also be the time of the marriage rites. This period, known as keplö kesi (fufu prohibited), ends when the groom brings the marriage payment to the father and a meal known as keplö kenai (fufu made) is prepared by the girl and her friends. Throughout the period of keplö kesi the future husband had until recently as a betrothal service to carry water every day for the mother from a nearby stream and to bring the father a daily calabash of palm wine. This former Ngkpani practice is well known to Umor men who said it had never applied in their village where, although gifts of palm wine to the father-in-law are made, these have always been occasional while water carrying is regarded in Umor as a woman's task.

There is both an appropriate age for betrothal and an appropriate period for its duration but these are not adhered to rigidly. It is generally considered that a girl is ready for betrothal at the second harvest after the beginning of puberty as indicated by her first menstruation, and the customary time for the declaration of a betrothal is at the end of the main yam harvest in November or December. The marriage rites should then be carried out at the end of the second harvest following, making four years in all from puberty. But apart from other contingencies which may affect its duration the occurrence of pregnancy during betrothal frequently, as will be shown, reduces the length of the period.

Synopses of two premarital histories will illustrate shortened and extended betrothal periods. Isū in Idjiman ward in Umor was betrothed to Obasi also of Idjiman in December, two harvests after the time when she first menstruated. Obasi rendered farm clearing services to his prospective father-in-law during the following February or March and Isū had become pregnant by this time. As a result of her pregnancy the marriage rites were performed according to custom before the end of the sixth moon of her pregnancy i.e. before the harvest of that year and her child was born during harvest time. She remained in her mother's household as is customary, until her husband had built a woman's house for his wife which was completed only after another seven or eight months just before the next harvest so that the new household did not function as an economic unit until the following farming year. In this instance the marriage ceremony took place approximately two and a half years after puberty, and the family was established as an independent economic unit with the opening of the farming year three and a half years after puberty. Assuming the latter to have occurred at between eleven and twelve years of age then the bride was less than sixteen years of age when she came to live with her husband.

Djasi of Biko Biko ward became betrothed to Otū of Ukpakapi during the planting season. She had first reached puberty three harvests before that time. Otū made gifts to her and her parents during the Lebokū festival of the first year of the betrothal, but it was not until the second year that he and his age mates performed services for his prospective father-in-law. In this instance the services were in house building and not in farm work. Djasi planted a groundnut patch in that year. In the previous year she had not done this but had obtained from her mother the groundnuts which she presented to Otū. During part of the Lebokū festival of the next year, a time when the love affairs and night parties of the young girls of Umor rise to a crescendo, Otū went to Calabar with an older man on a trading trip and learned after his return that Djasi has accepted a gift from a youth Ubi of his own patriclan in Ukpakapi ward, who had joined her in a night party of her age mates. Otū angrily tackled Ubi, accusing him of betrayal of an age-set fellow and a kinsman, and abused Djasi for her unfaithfulness, not only to her face but among his friends and hers! Djasi refused to receive Otū again and said she would be betrothed to Ubi. Otū demanded repayment for the presents and services he had performed to her and her parents but was refused. He went to the head of his ward to demand that repayment should be made. Custom was in his favour here for a father should reimburse a suitor who has given the betrothal gifts and services if the girl or her parents later wilfully refuse the marriage. But in this case he lacked the support of the elders of his own patriclan. It was said that no one got to the bottom of lovers' quarrels and as the girl was coming to live in the dwelling area of the patriclan as a wife in either case it was not good to continue the quarrel. The value set on clan solidarity appears to have overriden the undoubted merits of a case which would in the ordinary way have been pressed by the clan head. Djasi's marriage ceremony, which was to have been performed after the harvest of that year, was postponed until the following year when Ubi was the bridegroom. In this instance six years elapsed between the onset of puberty and the marriage rites while it would be a further year before the wife joined her husband to found an independent household.

Pregnancy before **Betrothal**. Girls rarely become pregnant before betrothal. In such a situation there is nearly always a youth ready to take the girl as his wife and if she has several lovers they may dispute over the right. There are, however, occasions in which the father of the girl is left to discover the identity of her lover, and to visit his father or other patrilineal kinsman to insist on the youth's obligation to provide marriage money and take her as a wife after the birth of the child.

CHAPTER IV

IV THE MARRIAGE RITES

The first marriage of a Yakö girl involves a series of distinct
ceremonial acts which are dovetailed in a continuous sequence.They are
the announcements of the marriage, the gathering of the marriage firewood (ngbö mun), offerings to the matriclan shrines,the clitorodectomy
rite (kūkpot), the wedding feasts (ebon keta), the transfer of the
marriage payment (libeman) and finally the seclusion of the bride
(okpolökpölo). The character of these separate ceremonial elements can
be appreciated only from a descriptive account in which their overlapping stages are made clear. They are connected overtly by the fact
that the organisers and main participants, namely the age mates of the
bride, of her father, of her mother and of the bridegroom, are the
same throughout.

It has already been pointed out that the Yakö consider the appropriate time for the marriage rites to be the second harvest following that at which betrothal occurred. But the proposal that marriage
rites should be undertaken at a particular harvest should come not from
the groom or the bride's parents but from the age mates of the latter.
When a girl has a lover who has declared himself to her parents, the
age mates of the mother come to her at the next harvest time bringing
a calabash of palm wine and say 'Your daughter is growing up.Next harvest it will be time for her to have kekpopam.' The mother should by
convention demur, saying that her daughter is too young. In fact if
she really considered this so she would not have agreed to recognise
the betrothal. The father tells his closest age set friend of this
and his age mates follow suit a few days later. Kekpopam is the term
for one form of the clitorodectomy rite, known as kūkpot,which is held
only at the end of the harvest season. The term is derived from kūkpot + kepam = edge, and indicates that the operation is performed at
sites, each special to one patriclan in the uncultivated land at the
edge of the village. Kekpopam is the standard and preferred form of
the rite but it cannot be carried out if the girl is already pregnant.
Kūkpot must then be performed in the bush (likōt) remote from the village at a site known as likpöbö of which there is in Umor one for each
of the four wards. The rite is then termed likpökōt (kūkpot + likōt)
and carried out during the seventh moon of pregnancy no matter when in
the year that may fall.

The Announcements of the Marriage. After the yam planting following the declarations of the parents' age mates,in April or May the
father goes or sends to one of the forest villages to the east of Yakö
territory where game is abundant to buy a smoked antelope carcase (kemen)
and tells his wife to arrange with her friends for the preparation of

a large supply of fufu on the next kokö day.[1]

He calls his age mates in the evening of aiyo-kokö to inspect the
meat and they ask the girl's mother to make some oil sauce to eat with
the neck of the kemen. On the same evening they tell all the members
of the father's age-set and other friends of his in all four wards to
come to his compound in the morning on the next day,after their return
from tapping their palm trees, each bringing his calabash of wine. The
father has given a large supply of yams, forty or so, to his wife and
these will be made into fufu by her friends on that day.

For the feast on kokö all the invited men assemble during the morning and there will be thirty or forty present if the father is popular.
Large calabash bowls of fufu are set out together with small bowls of
sauce. This is eaten first and then a large wine pot is produced and
filled by the friends from their calabashes.The father's 'true friend'
(otūmō monowō), i.e. his closest declared friend among his age mates,
who takes charge of the proceedings, brings out one front leg of the
kemen with oil sauce. This is shared and eaten before drinking. After
drinking the guests will ask the father to bring out the rest of the
meat and he tells his 'true friend' to do so.The latter then announces
what all in fact know already "The reason I call all you people today
is to tell you that in the coming harvest our daughter will have kekpopam. She will collect firewood and then kūkpot will be done for her."

---

[1] Kokö is a term for one of the days in the six day week at Umor. The
days are:-
    aiyo-kokö = before kokö;
    kokö;
    kokö-blokö = kokö passed;
    aiyo-ōpongōbi = before ōpongōbi;
    ōpongōbi;
    ōpongōbi-blokö = ōpongōbi passed.
Kokö is the day of the main market in Umor. It is also the day appropriate for most rituals and celebrations whether for the whole village
or for smaller groups. On this day people leave the village for only
short periods if possible and visiting of all kinds takes place. Ōpongōbi is the day of the smaller weekly market and is particularly associated with ritual activities connected with women. Thus a man must
be buried on kokö but a woman on ōpongōbi.
The same cycle is found at Nkō and Ngkpani while the two other
Yakö villages Ekuri and Idomi have, in common with the riverside Ekumuru,
a four day week with only one market. In this shorter week, however,
the kokö day has the same significance as at Umor.

If there are not too many people the father's friend will keep back one leg of meat to be eaten later by their age mates alone. Otherwise the father will have to buy an extra back leg for them to eat on the next day (kokö-blökö) when each member brings one yam, to be given to the girl's mother to make them fufu, and one bottle of palm wine. On this occasion no formal speeches are made.

Later in the year after the Lebokü rites the mother gives a similar feast for her friends also on a kokö day with a second feast for her age mates.

Gathering the Marriage Firewood. When the main yam harvest begins in early November the bride has to collect the marriage firewood (mbö mun). With a large specially made 'firewood head pad' (lekumika) and a flat piece of wood to serve as a firewood carrying plank (kemuntipa) she goes to her parents' and their friends farms to collect yam vine poles. She should have worked at hoeing up yam hills at planting time for friends of her mother so that they will now give her some of their yam poles in return. She seeks the aid of her age mates and of other girls in her patriclan who have not yet had kükpot, and two or more girls who are going to have kekpopam at this harvest may join forces. The bridegroom should provide the bride with a matchet, fibre rope and the carrying plank and come with his age mates and other friends to the farm in which she is collecting to help chop up the wood into suitable lengths. This firewood cutting and carrying goes on intermittently for about a month as the harvests are gathered in until a hundred or more stout poles three or four inches in diameter and over five foot long have been collected together in a pile on the farming path near the entrance to the village.

The groom and his friends now erect a low timber frame in the compound of the bride's father on which the wood is to be piled. The frame is three or four yards across and five or six feet deep. The bridegroom has to organise a party for piling the wood on a kokö day. He announces this in advance and is helped both by his age set and also by patriclan fellows, including older men such as his own father and his friends. As the wood has already been carried to the outskirts of the village it can be brought in quickly with a flourish on this day. The bride's age mates also assemble in the compound and as the work proceeds in the morning the girls try to impede the work by playfully dragging wood away. (See fig.2).

When the job is done the girl go off to fetch water from a spring and take it to the compound of the groom, where the men all bathe. The girls then return to the bride's house where they shell and boil groundnuts and also cook yams in oil. They fill two large bowls with these and take them to the groom's compound. The yams are supplied by the

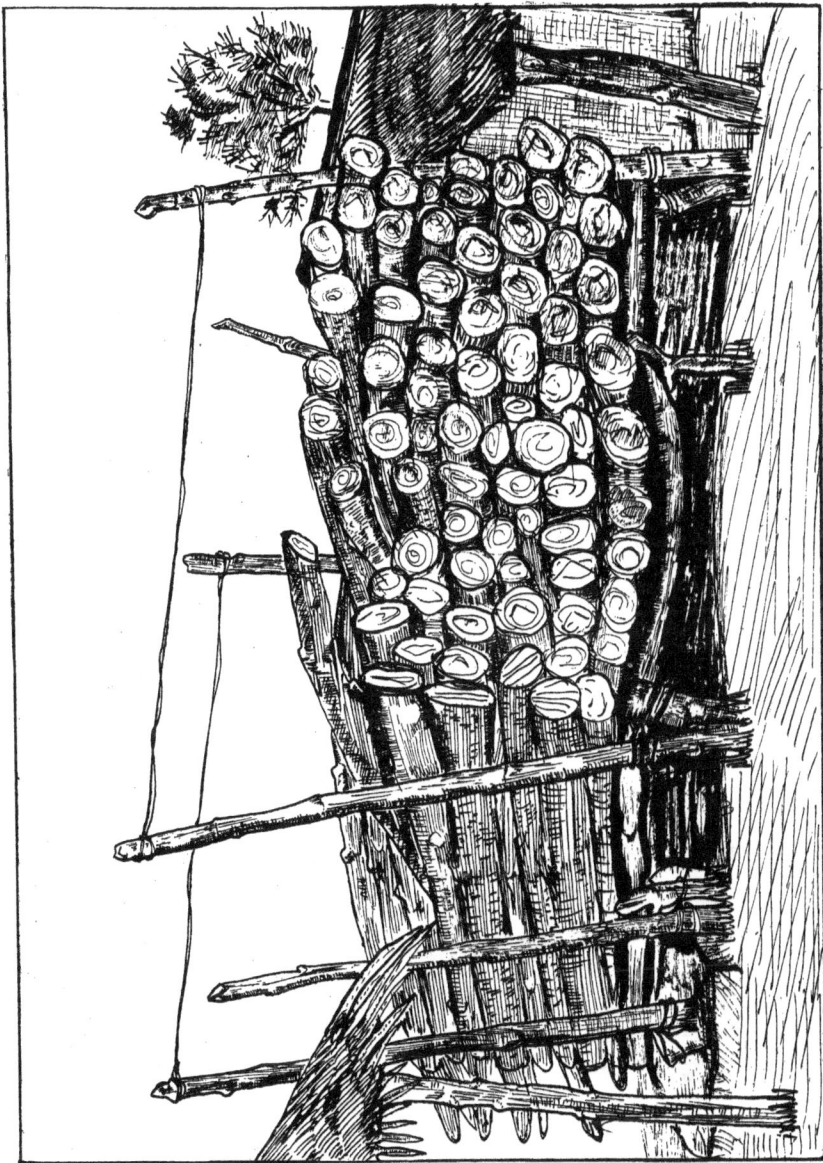

Fig. 2. The Marriage Firewood.

bride's mother; the groundnuts should have been specially grown by the
bride in her parents' farm. In the groom's compound his patriclan fellows have meanwhile brought palm wine in the evening and his fatherpro-
vides a smoked leg of antelope (kemen) for him. All this food is set
out as a feast for the youths and men who took part in the firewood piling. This is the first occasion on which the groom and his father publicly indicate the forthcoming marriage and this feast is regarded as
an announcement to the patriclan of the groom and his father. On the
next aiyo-kokö the father of the bride calls his age mates together and
announces "Tomorrow I wish you to take our daughter to all ase",and the
mother calls her age mates to make the same announcement. The ase(sing.
yose) are the spirit shrines of the matriclans of which there are eleven
in Umor. Both the groups assemble in the compound next morning soon
after dawn and join together to escort the bride. The parents stay behind in their compound.

Offerings to the Ase. The priests (bi'ina) of the several ase
will not have been warned in advance, but they have to be in their compounds on every kokö and they know that this is the season forsuch rites.
The party sets out in a file with the father's friends going in front
of the bride who is followed by her own age mates with some of the age
mates of the mother behind. There may be twenty or more people in the
procession.

The bride wears a large cloth arranged as a bustle, a necklet of
precious beads and an ivory bangle. Her father's 'true friend' carries
a narrow necked 'yidunsüwo' pot of palm wine, another carries a larger
calabash of wine and a third a piece of smoked antelope meat on a small
wooden meat plate. The ase are visited in no fixed order save that those
situated in the ward of the bride are reached last. At first only the
friends of the bride's father go with the priest into the miniature house
which contains the yose shrine. An assistant (ntakatüm) of the priest
cuts up a portion of the meat and pours some of the wine from the pot
into a calabash cup. After four pieces of meat have been placed before
the yose and a drop of wine has been poured into a drinking horn which
forms part of it all the men eat a piece of meat and drink some wine.
Meanwhile the priest addresses the yose: "This is meat for you and this
is palm wine for you. This girl has come to smear chalk as she wants
kükpot" but he makes no verbal request of the yose. After wine has been
drunk the priest powders a stick of chalk on a stone in front of the yose
and mixes with it the wine put in the horn. He next smears himself and
then the close friends of the bride's father on the chest.This mixing
of a paste of chalk and wine which is smeared on the body of the priest,
the supplicants and others present, is carried out at every ceremony at

a yose shrine.[1] The bride and the other women who have remained at the entrance to the compound are now called in to approach the yose. The priest first smears the bride vertically on the chest, on the forehead, on sides of head, over the shoulders and then right round the body above waist. She then puts out both palms and the priest blows on them and says "Be in good health" (wotö litawō). The friends of the mother then enter the tiny yose house by ones and twos and they are smeared with chalk in the same way and they are followed by the friends of the bride. The bridegroom is not present and has no part in this ceremony, save that he should have provided the palm wine to be taken to the yose.

After all these have been visited in this way the party returns to the bride's compound where the father gives a leg of smoked keman meat and wine to his age mates and the mother similarly gives meat and wine to the women. Both these groups send for more wine and stay for most of the morning talking and drinking. But the bride's age mates do not stay, and the bride herself, having cut a piece of smoked meat into very small pieces which she puts in a bowl, goes round the village offering pieces of the meat to all her acquaintances announcing "The next aiyo-koko̱ I shall make kukpot." She should go right round the village - alone or with one or at most two of her friends.

From this day she may not bathe until after the rite has been performed five days later, and is expected to behave capriciously to the groom, trying to avoid him, while he for his part must try to track her down. The bride is free to invite another youth to join her with her age mates at night if she can escape the bridegroom, but it appeared that, if she is anxious to marry the groom, she will only make a pretence of this.

On the next ōpongōbi or ōpongōbi-blökö one or two of the father's friends go to the ōmanamaña to ask her to perform the clitorodectomy taking a gift of a small piece of smoked meat, sauce and palm wine. In Umor there is an ōmanamana in each of the four wards. They have to be chosen from the matriclans connected with the four ase Ōdjokōbi, Obolene, Esukpa

---

[1] This chalk is, according to the Yakö, dug by women of Ngūsū in Edda country on the west bank of the Cross River. They sell it at ninepence a headload at Ngūsū to women from Afikpo and elsewhere. The Afikpo women pound it up, mix it with water and mould it into biconical sticks about two inches long. These sticks are sold in the Afikpo and riverside markets, whence Yakö supplies come, at ten to twenty for a penny. Every priest and magician among the Yakö and their neighbours uses this chalk to smear supplicants and sacred objects.

and Obot Lokōna. The senior ōmanamana plays a prominent part in the annual harvest fertility rites in Umor, but their main function is the performance of clitoridectomy. When a new appointment has to be made the village head, the village speaker and the ina of Obolene make the choice after consulting the other yamanamana and a ritual of induction is performed by the village head at the yose Ōdjokōbi of which he is priest. The new ōmanamana is then instructed by one of the others until she is skilled.

If the parents of a bride are divorced they are expected to come together and to co-operate in friendly fashion at the marriage of their daughter. The bride will usually have passed her childhood with her mother since the divorce, but both are expected to return to the father's compound for the clitoridectomy rite and the feasts which follow. Sometimes, however, particularly when the mother has gone to live in another village the father goes with his age set friends to the mother's compound. In either case a rite known as kewipi (water spitting) which enjoins friendly behaviour on the parties is performed on the arrival of the divorced party. In the father's compound this rite should be directed by the head of his patrilineage (ūwo womon = our father) who brings a calabash of water, sets it down on the ground and powders into it a stick of chalk. He then sucks up some of the water and sprays it over the extended hands of the bride saying "From today, when we spit water on her, we are all in peace together." He then invites the father and the mother and their companions to do the same.

The Clitoridectomy rite. On aiyo-kokö, the day of the clitoridectomy rite, all the head hair, save for an occipital patch, and the pubic hair of the bride are shaved off by a friend of the girl's mother and a message is sent to the ōmanamana of the ward who comes to the entrance of the compound often accompanied by one of the other yamanamana as an assistant. They both wear only bark cloth bustles, the native clothing for the older women, and stand there silently, waiting. The father has told the friends of the girl's mother, who will accompany her, where the kekpopam site for his patriclan is and a procession is led by the best friend of the bride's mother who is followed by the two yamanamana, the bride, more friends of the mother and finally the age mates of the bride - no matter whether they themselves have had kūkpot or not. The bride wears a special narrow girdle (eponidja = marriage girdle) of undyed raphia from which a loose bundle of raphia fibre hangs down on one side (see Frontispiece).

On reaching the site a friend of the mother, who has brought a hoe, clears a space in which the bride lies on her back. She is held by the mother's friends; the others form a close ring round her and the ōmanamana operates immediately with a native razor (okōwa)1 and squeezes on to the

---

1 A knife with a lunate blade about four inches long. The operation is not usually severe. The sheath covering the clitoris proper is alone removed by a single transverse cut.

wound the juice of certain green leaves in which guinea grains, which she has chewed then and there, have been placed. No dressing is placed on the wound. Two of the mother's friends have brought a pot of water and a bowl; and water is poured with which the ōmanamana bathes the bride while a small hole is dug in which the clitoris sheath is buried. The bride is then rubbed all over with red camwood powder by the ōmanamana who also rubs camwood on her own body and on one arm and one leg of each of the bride's age mates and on the leg of other women present. The procession is re-formed to return to the bride's compound. The closest friend of the bride precedes her carrying a bowl of camwood from which she sprinkles the powder on the path. The ōmanamana and her assistant leave them to return to their own houses immediately. Later in the day, a friend of the mother brings the ōmanamana a gift of one shilling – before the introduction of coinage from five to ten rods and later until the recent depression several shillings were expected – twenty yams and a calabash of palm wine, all of which have been provided by the father.

On returning to the compound the bride is made to sit on the bed platform in her mother's house. The age mates of the groom who have been waiting in his compound are then summoned and they, but not the groom, arrive each carrying several young, light-green oil palm fronds. On arrival they split the fronds along the midribs and tie them to posts across the head of the platform to form a screen (yetōlokōlo) closing it in while the bride remains inside. They joke with her and among themselves about the operation saying "We heard you cry very loud. How is the wound?". On their return to the groom's compound he hands them a present for the bride known as kebō kali (= stop crying) consisting of two calabashes of palm wine, four coconuts, two shillings (formerly four or more rods) and a bundle of raphia fibre. These they give to the bride's friends while she herself peeps through the screen of palm fronds. The raphia fibre is to be used for the bride's girdle. One coconut is to be placed between her legs to protect the wound. The others are for her friends.

Handing over the Marriage Money. The marriage payment or "bride wealth" which the Yakō call marriage money (libeman, from mbo = marriage and liman = currency (rods or coinage)) is usually sent with these gifts. Until a decade or so ago, it was customary in Umor to make the marriage payment on a kokō day previous to the day of kūkpot when the bride's parents and her age mates were told to await the bridegroom's age mates in their compound. The transfer of the libeman was then marked by formalities which are no longer observed. The groom's age mates first offered the money to the bride's mates who refused it pretending that the bridegroom had not made betrothal gifts saying "No, we cannot take marriage money from you, you have never given our friend anything not even threepence, nor a penny not a halfpenny nor even a bundle of raphia fibre (yititangpa)". Whereupon the leaders of the groom's friends produces these very things saying: "To show that our friend is ready to do everything you expect here is threepence and a penny

and a halfpenny and yititangpa." The libeman is then offered again and
accepted. The same conventional phrase is used by a wife after marriage
when replying angrily to a complaint or reproach. Irrespective of the facts
she will say: "What do I owe to you; what have you given me, not even
threepence nor a penny nor a halfpenny nor even yititangpa."

In Umor the etiquette in offering the marriage money has now changed.
It is rarely if ever offered until the day of kūkpot. The convention now
is to offer the kebō kali on that day as described above and this is at
first refused because the libeman has not already been given. The bride's
friends say "Where is the libeman; you should bring it with the kebō kali.
This palm wine too is not enough, many people have come here.We shall keep
this, but we want four more calabashes of wine." The spokesman among the
groom's friends then protests that the libeman will be brought at once, or
within such and such a time as the case may be, and presses the kebō kali
gift on the bride's friends. He then goes back with his companions,to in-
form the groom and his father, who know quite well what they are going to
say and will usually provide at least part of the marriage money for the
youths to take to the bride's compound. If, as sometimes happens today,
they send back the youths with only a promise of future payment,the bride's
friends will usually send back the kebō kali, save for the wine,saying that
it should be sent later when the marriage money is actually handed over.

When the marriage money is handed over on the day of kūkpot it is
given to the bride's age mates who hand it to her father and he makes them
a gift of a few shillings from it then and there. If it is transferred later it is handed direct to the bride's father by the groom himself or his
father who is accompanied by a few friends as witnesses. The character of
the Yakö marriage payment, the ways in which it is amassed by or on behalf
of the groom,and how it is disposed of will be considered later.

After handing over the libeman the age mates of the bridegroom return
to his compound where others of his age set and many of his patriclan fellows have assembled. The bridegroom, or his father, provides a back leg
of smoked meat while his mother has cooked oil sauce and several bowls of
fufu. All taking part either bring wine, or provide 1d for it to be bought.
Patriclan fellows of the groom are expected to give him a present of yams
and money ranging from one to five yams and 3d. The bride's age mates later return to the groom's compound, bring a return gift for the kebō kali
consisting of some meat and sauce, and one shilling provided by the bride.
This feast of the age set and patriclan fellows of the groom is quite distinct from the protracted marriage feast in the bride's compound.

The Wedding Feasts. In the meantime a few friends of the mother who
did not go with the bride for the clitorodectomy operation have been preparing a large supply of fufu for the first of the feasts of ebon keta (=
marriage visiting). For this a store of yams had been set aside at harvest

time. The bride's mother should have a supply of 100 yams for her friends. The father should have a similar supply of 100 yams for his friends in his man's house. The bride's friends are also given about 50 yams by the bride's father for their own use. In all about ten sticks of medium sized yams are required for the marriage feasts. All the supplies of yams are brought in and laid out in the houses before the day of the ceremony. The three groups of age mates go out to the family yam stack for this purpose and carry in the yams; young boys of their patriclans usually accompany the father's age mates to do their carrying. This occasion is called mbȯngpʊ (=mbʊ̈, marriage and mpʊ̈ = yam stack) and on this day the father provides a smoked back leg of antelope, and his two closest friends, one front leg each, for a feast. The mother and two friends of hers do the same, and the food is eaten by the two groups sitting separately after their return to the compound. Both sets produce their own palm wine. The yams are set out in rows of neat heaps of five on the inner platform of the houses which are to be occupied by the participants in the marriage feast.

On the day of kūkpot (aiyo-kokʊ̈) the mother's age mates first make fufu with some of the father's yams for his friends. After that they cook some of the mother's yams for themselves. The bride's age mates cook for themselves from their own supply. The father and mother each give one back leg of antelope to their respective friends and a smaller piece of meat to the bride's friends which is eaten after the fufu.

The age mates of the groom receive forty yams and a stick of dried fish from his father on this day and take these to the girl's compound and give it to her friends for them to make fufu daily for the youths until the following kokʊ̈ but one, in seven days time. This fufu is cooked in the night and carried in two or more fufu bowls to the groom's compound just before dawn. During this period the youths sleep in the groom's compound. Similarly the age mates of the bride, of her father and of her mother all sleep in the parents' compound until the second kokʊ̈. The bride occupies her mother's house which her age mates also use. The mother with her age mates obtain the temporary use of another woman's house in the compound, while the father and his friends occupy his own house. The mother's age mates get up before dawn each morning and cook fufu and stew for themselves and the father's friends (friends of father provide their own meat for stew).

The bride's father gives her one back leg of kemen and two shillings when she returns from the clitorodectomy rite. When on this or subsequent days the friends and relatives, to whom the bride has announced the ceremony by giving pieces of meat, come to greet her after the rite, giving a small present such as ½d. or 1d, she cuts off a sliver from the meat and offers it to them.

Towards the evening of this day the groom leaves the further arrangement of food distribution in his compound to his closest friend and comes to the bride's compound to salute her, first asking formally "awongke kŭk-pot; kŭkpot kow kodea?" (= you return from clitoridectomy; (your) clitori-dectomy how is it?). She is expected to reply briefly and without concern saying for example "Bom bom, kōdö" (= something, nothing, i.e. It is of no matter, I am not upset about it) or "kŭkpot koninom" (= kŭkpot is painful).

The bride must continue to remain behind the screen and when the groom comes she may put only her head through and he stays a few minutes. He can however, return later in the evening to spend the night with her, going in-side the screen.

Early the next morning as dawn is breaking the bride's age mates make fufu and take it to the groom's mates and come away, the mother's age mates similarly take fufu and stew to the age mates of the bride's father. In the morning and again in the evening on each day until the next kokö the age mates of the groom and of the bride's father come to their compounds when returning from tapping their oil palms for wine and stop there to drink and gossip. Otherwise every one goes about his own affairs.

On the kokö seven days after the clitoridectomy rite the bride's age mates cook fufu for the groom's age mates for the last time but the mother's mates continue to prepare it in the early morning for those of the father for another six days until the following kokö. On that day the presentation of gifts to the father and mother of the bride begins. The gifts are brought by the age mates and other friends of the father and mother on one or other of the days from this kokö to the next. In recent years the closest friend of the father has been expected to give 2/-, 40 yams and palm wine. The second friend should give 1/6 and 20 or 30 yams and palm wine; from other members of his koboma 1/6 to 1/- with 20 yams and palm wine is expected; less in-timate friends bring 6d and 15 yams or 3d and 10 yams and palm wine. From every gift one yam is set aside to provide fufu for a further feast. The number of friends bringing gifts to the bride's father in this way will vary from about twenty to over fifty with his popularity. They will include mem-bers of his age-set, of his patriclan, of his matriclan and other friends both young and old.

The amounts of the gifts have been fairly stable in recent years but were said to have been much higher a generation ago. Always, however, if the bride's father has already made a marriage gift of this kind to a friend on a previous occasion that friend should make a larger money gift than he re-ceived. In the past he would have been expected to give several rods more than he received. At present from 3d to 1/- more in cash is expected of him.

The bride's father hands over the gifts of money to his closest friend who also takes the reserved yams. These are used in a feast which is held on the kokö following that on which the presentation of gifts has ended. The

friends of the bride's mother bring presents to her in the same way during these days. I was told that the gifts by women to the mother should
be larger than those which his friends give to the father and that in
the prosperous years of the recent time the mother's closest friend was
expected to give from ten shillings or more with fifty to a hundred yams
and that three or four shillings was expected from all her age mates.
The actual amounts were, however, considerably less during my stay among
the Yakö, on account mainly of the slump of palm oil prices, and my impression was that women's gifts to the bride's mother were at that time
smaller not larger than those to the father. I was not able to obtain a
full list of wedding gifts for a representative series of marriages, but
at the wedding feasts for the daughter of a man of about 35 years of age
with a medium sized farm which occurred during my later period of field
work the father received a total of £1.2.0 in cash from about forty friends
and the mother about 18/- from about thirty friends. The closest friend
of the father gave 2/6 and twenty-five yams while the mother's closest
friend gave 1/6 and fifteen yams.

The yams set aside by the closest friends of the father and mother
are cooked and made into fufu for the feast on kökö. The custodians of
the gifts also use part of the money received to buy meat for the feast.
In the case referred to above the father's friend used 7/- to buy three
legs of smoked antelope (kemen) and three legs of smoked bush pig and
other meat and ten calabashes of palm wine. This meat was shared by the
forty or so men friends who came to the feast.

The obligation to reciprocate these wedding gifts, or more exactly
respond with a gift larger than one has received is very strongly maintained by the Yakö. Men and women will, if they lack the means themselves, borrow money and yams from their matrikin in order to make the
appropriate gifts. On the other hand if of two close friends one has
more daughters than the other the father or mother with many daughters
will tell the friend that the gift should be small since there will be
several wedding feasts in their household.

The feast following the offering of gifts to the parents of the
bride concludes the wedding ceremonies and the sequence and duration of
the marriage feasts from the day of kükpot are thus:-

Aiyo-kokö	Kokö	Kokö	Kokö	Kokö	Kokö
Kükpot First feast to age mates of bride and her parents. Feast to age mates and patriclan friends of bridegroom.	Fufu cooked for bride's parents' age mates Fufu cooked for groom's age mates by bride's age mates		Gifts to parents of bride by age mates, kinsmen and other friends	Final marriage feast for all friends of bride's parents.	

The palm leaf screen before the bride's bed is left in position until it has withered and is then taken down by the bride's age mates and thrown away in the bush near the village.

Marriage Rites for a Pregnant Bride. If, as has already been mentioned, a girl becomes pregnant before the harvest at which it was intended to carry out the clitoridectomy rite the circumstances and character of these ceremonies are modified, unless, as is sometimes attempted, the girl with or without the connivance of her mother is able to conceal her pregnancy until harvest time. The clitoridectomy rite, which is then known as likpokŏt is held in the sixth moon of pregnancy at a particular site in the bush set aside for this purpose of which at Umor there is one for every ward.

Before likpokŏt a pregnant bride is taken by her mother and her mother's brother or other close matrikinsman to the fertility shrine of their matriclan. They bring an offering and the priest prays for her health during pregnancy and successful childbirth. This is distinct from the rite before kekpopam in which all the matriclan shrines are visited, and is a separate rite of appeal for safe delivery which would otherwise be performed after the marriage when the bride eventually became pregnant. The preliminary rite of piling the marriage firewood is also omitted, while the wedding feasts are curtailed.

The likpokŏt rite itself must be performed on an ŏpongŏbi-blŏkŏ not a kokŏ day. The father and mother of the bride give a feast on that day to their age mates and other close friends and to those of the bride, but the friends of the bride and her parents do not stay on in the compound. The groom's age mates should bring the kebʊ kali gift and the marriage payment after the party return from the clitoridectomy rite, but no palm frond screen is set up by the groom's friends round the bride's bed, nor do the bride's friends daily visit the groom and his friends to take fufu, they merely reciprocate the kebʊ kali gift on the day of the rite. The friends of the parents will come to their compound to greet them bringing wine to drink on the days following and one by one will offer their marriage gifts. Before two kokŏ days have passed the second feast is provided with part of the gifts received. But neither the gifts nor the feast are on so considerable a scale as for a kekpopam marriage. Unless the father has himself previously given a particular friend a gift for a kekpopam marriage and has himself no other daughter who may be expected to have a kekpopam wedding in the future the friend is expected to give only half of what he would had it been a kekpopam and not a likopokŏt wedding.

CHAPTER V

ANALYSIS OF MARRIAGE RITES

The full series of rituals, feasts and gifts which mark the establishment of marital status may be summarised as follows:

FIRST HARVEST AFTER BETROTHAL. Proposal of clitoridectomy to be held at next harvest by mother's age mates.

NEXT CULTIVATING TIME. Father's feast given to his age mates (koboma) announcing the forthcoming clitoridectomy.

Mother's feast given likewise to her age mates.

SECOND HARVEST TIME

Marriage Firewood collected. The bride and her age mates aided by the groom and his age mates collect yam poles for firewood in farms of her parents and their friends.

Firewood stacked, on a koko̎ by groom, his age set and patriclan friends, on a frame in the bride's compound. The bride then sends a gift of cooked yams and groundnuts to the groom and friends for a feast in his compound.

Visit to bride's parents' yam stack; to obtain about ten sticks of yams for the marriage feasts to follow kekpopam, the clitoridectomy rite. The yams are displayed in the parents' houses.

AIYO-KOKO̎. Rites at the matriclan shrines ·(ase) - parents' age mates take the bride to all ase in turn. Meat is offered, water is poured on bride's hands and her health is sought from each spirit by its priest.

Bride announces her clitoridectomy - visiting all her acquaintances and offering meat.

NEXT KOKO̎. The marriage money was formerly handed with yititangpagift by groom's friends to bride's friends for her father.

NEXT ŌPONGŪBI. The ōnanamana is requested to operate by the father's friends on the next aiyo-koko̎.

NEXT AIYO-KOKO̎. Clitoridectomy performed.

Kebō kali (crying stopped). Bride on returning from the clitoridectomy rite is visited in her house by some of groom's age mates who erect screen of young palm fronds round the bed in which she remains secluded.

They report completion of kekpopam to the groom who sends them with the kebo̅ kali gift to the bride. This should now be accompanied or immediately followed by the marriage payment.

Bride's friends demand marriage money (if necessary) and when it is brought they hand it to the father who makes them a gift.

Groom gives a feast to his age set and patriclan fellows in his compound all of whom give wine and patriclan fellows yams or a few pence.

Bride sends a gift to the groom of meat and one shilling.

Groom's age mates receive 40 yams and meat or fish from groom'sfather and takes these to bride's compound for her age mates to use daily in preparing food for them until the ko̅ko̅ seven days later.

Feasts for age mates of bride and her parents from yams and smoked meat provided by parents and cooked by mother's and bride's mates, each group sitting separately and bringing their own wine. Bride's age mates prepare their own food from yams supplied by father. All three groups of age mates spend the night in the compound, each group in a separate house.Her father gives the bride smoked meat and a shilling, the former to be offered to the relatives and acquaintances who will visit her.

The groom visits the bride in the evening and passes the night with her behind the frond screen.

UNTIL THE THIRD KOKŐ AFTER CLITORIDECTOMY. The bride's friends cook fufu and stew before dawn the next morning (koko) and take it to the groom and friends. This continues daily until the next kokő i.e. for seven mornings in all.

Parents' age mates bring in wine in the morning and evening to the bride's compound and stay to join in drinking and sleep in the compound.

Mother's age mates cook fufu and stew before dawn and take it to father and his friends. This continues daily until the third kokő i.e.for thirteen mornings in all.

The bride's kinsfolk and acquaintances visit her to bring small gifts of money and receive a token slice of meat from her and wine from the parents.

FROM THE THIRD TO THE FOURTH KOKŐ.

Parents' friends and kinsfolk relatives bring them marriage gifts,consisting of yams and money varying in amount according to closeness of friendship and the obligation to exceed gifts previously received from the parents at marriages of their own daughters. Some twenty to fifty friends and relatives will bring gifts.

FIFTH KOKÖ AFTER KŪKPOT.

Father's and mother's last feasts to their friends using some of the yams and money received as gifts. The food is prepared by the mother's friends.

Several of the implications of elements in this sequence including the transfer of marriage money will be considered later in detail. It is in the meantime necessary to appreciate the general character of the social relations that they express. The most remarkable feature of the Yakö marriage ceremonial is the emphasis on the relations of the chief participants to their age mates and the lack of emphasis on their relations to either kinship groups or particular circles of kinsmen. The activities centre on the bride, her father, her mother and the bridegroom. At practically every stage the initiative is taken by an age mate of one of these parties to the marriage, while the other participants or supporters consist of other friends mostly of the age set of the party concerned of which the small group of age mates (the koboma or letekö) is at least the nucleus.

This emphasis applies more particularly to the activities of the bride and her parents. While age mates are again prominent in activities undertaken by or on behalf of the bridegroom, members of his patriclan of all ages are expected to take part in the firewood piling rite and also in the feast given by the groom in his compound on the day of kūkpot. There may, and generally will be, among the age mates of the groom and among those of the bride's father, several members of their respective patrilineages and clans but it is as age mates and not as kinsmen that they associate with the father or the groom on these occasions, and this is also true for the age mates of the bride and her mother.

Neither the matrilineal nor the patrilineal kin of the bride or of the groom are as social groups concerned in the marriage rituals. The patriclans of the bride and groom have an interest in maintaining the exogamic rule which would be sustained by the intervention of the clan head (Obot Kepūn) and elders if an infraction threatened, but they give no ceremonial group approval of the marriage. The matriclans of the bride and the groom have no corporate relation whatever to the marriage ceremonies while the matrilineage of the bride although it has, as will be seen, an interest in the maintenance of the marriage once established nevertheless takes no part in its ceremonial recognition. It is only after the ceremonies have ended that the mother's brother of the bride approaches her father to claim a portion of the marriage money.

It is further to be noted that the ritual acts are all connected directly with the changing status of the bride and not with that of the groom. No ritual acts, corresponding to the firewood piling, the visits to the ase shrines, the bride's announcement of clitorodectomy and the clitorodectomy rite itself, are carried out to mark the change of status of the groom. This applies, moreover, not merely to the rites during this short period in which the marital relation is established and celebrated. There is a subsequent series of ritual acts to be considered later which again mark the changed status of the bride, but not that of the husband. These include a period of seclusion of the bride, during which she is distinctively costumed, at the end of which she makes a ceremonial circuit of certain sacred sites in the village, and also rituals to promote fertility and safe delivery of her child.

Yakö marriage ritual is thus primarily an expression of the passage of a nubile girl to the status of wife and prospective mother, and it is followed by rituals to promote fertility and avert the , dangers of childbirth. But with this ritual expression of the marital status of the bride are combined social activities of a different order. One is the transfer of marriage money which establishes the contractual obligations of the bride to the groom and will be analysed in a later section. The other is the celebration by the several parties to the marriage with their respective age mates, kinsfolk and other friends of the performance of these ritual and contractual acts.

These celebrations are not joint but several, and they differ in character and duration. Each party to the marriage gives feasts to his or her own age mates while the bride's age mates prepare a series of meals for the groom's age mates which symbolises her new obligations. The celebrations of the bride's parents are distinguished by considerable gifts to each parent from his or her age mates. The gifts at any particular marriage are but one set in a series which the members of this group of age mates make to one another in turn as their daughters marry for the first time. They have in the past been on an ascending scale, each successive gift being by custom greater than that which it reciprocates. This feature of Yakö wedding gifts, vaguely reminiscent as it is of competitive gift exchange in other societies and notably among the peoples of the North West Coast of America, has not in fact a markedly competitive character and there is no suggestion of humiliating the recipient of the gifts. It is probable that its development has been connected with an increasing abundance of currency first in rods and later in coinage during the recent past. On the other hand the reduction of currency in circulation during the last decade have in fact brought it to an end and wedding gifts of parents age mates have been falling not rising in amount.

CHAPTER VI

SECLUSION OF THE BRIDE

After a kekpopam ritual the bride goes into seclusion in her mother's house until the next harvest time or, if she becomes pregnant before then, until the fourth or fifth moon of pregnancy. A bride who is so secluded is known as ökpölökpöla (pl. yakpölökpöla). The seclusion is fairly strict; the bride is expected to spend the greater part of the day in one of the small cubicles (ekpoto, pl. ngpoto) otherwise used for storing food supplies, which are built on one or both sides of a Yakö woman's house. She may not go to farm, walk long distances or join dancing and other parties of her age mates. She may not go to the village bathing places but must wash in the house. She does no hard physical work but can and does cook food for herself and the household. Her age mates and other friends spend time with her gossiping and playing warri and she may in practice visit a nearby age mate or other friend who is also secluded. Visits to the latrine on the edge of the village are the only acceptable reasons for leaving the compound in which her mother's house is built, but one hears stories of secluded girls who manage to receive other lovers secretly at the houses of their friends and this is said to be the bride's retaliation if she thinks her husband is neglecting her.

A secluded bride is expected to eat plentifully and should be given more meat than is ordinarily available in a Yakö diet. Under these conditions of inaction and good feeding a bride usually becomes noticeably plumper after a few weeks and the English phrase used widely in Southern Nigeria for such seclusion, 'going into the fatting house', may be applied quite appropriately to the Yakö bride. The husband should visit her regularly and spend most nights with her. If he has no other wife and does not do this he will be suspected of other interests, especially if the marriage money has not been handed over. Early pregnancy is hoped for and it is explicitly believed that the ease and good living of this period of seclusion will help to promote it.

During this period of seclusion the bride wears a distinctive costume. Her hair is allowed to grow and is dressed in a series of spikes all over her head. Camwood paste which dries to a thick red powder covers her body and is renewed every few days. She wears a distinctive girdle known as kedjala, an inelastic ring about two inches thick made of pandanus root fibre bound with raphia which is also smeared with red camwood paste, and she carries or keeps by her side a knobbed stick studded with brass nails arranged in geometric patterns (see Frontispiece).

If a girl is already pregnant at the time of the clitoridectomy and wedding ceremonies she goes into seclusion only until the wound is healed which is usually not later than the third kokö after the wedding. During this period she paints herself with camwood but does not adopt the full costume of ŏkpŏlŏkpŏla wearing the girdle of loose raphia fibre used at the clitoridectomy for this period.

From the time of the marriage ceremonies, if the marriage money or the larger part of it has been duly handed over, the husband is regularly given meals by his wife in her mother's house although he works and passes most of his time in his own compound. Actually the mother of the wife provides the materials and may often cook the food. On most days the husband comes to his wife's mother's house for an evening meal and this is a recognised right while on each kokŏ or ŏpongŏbi day food is sent for him in the morning from the wife's house to his own compound. It is carried by any young girl available, not by the wife herself even if she is not secluded. The husband gets his other food in his parents' household. This practice like the wedding ceremonies so far described applies only when the wife is marrying for the first time.

Circuit of the Akōta. In Umor when the period of seclusion ends the bride has, before going freely about the village, to make a ritual circuit, visiting a number of sacred sites known as akōta (sing. likōta). There are twelve of these sites, each an inconspicuous heap of stone slabs, distributed somewhat unequally among the four wards. The bride is accompanied by her mother or another senior matrilineal kinswoman who carries a pot of water. On reaching each site she places one foot on the stones while the older woman sprinkles water from the pot on to the stones. Nothing is said and the pair move on at once to the next site. The akōta are not particularly associated with either marriage or childbirth. They are visited by all priests of the matrilineal clans on installation and also by members of the premier men's society, Ikpungkara, in both cases after a period of seclusion and when the other rites of admission have been completed. The visits to the akōta during a circuit of the village thus appear as a ritual ending of seclusion and an indication of the establishment of a new status, that of a married woman in which normal activities of daily life are now to be taken up.

If pregnancy does not occur during the year long period of seclusion following a kekpopam marriage the pregnancy rites to be considered later will follow and not precede the circuit of the akōta but otherwise this circuit concludes the series of rites following the first marriage of a Yako girl. She may, and normally will, continue to live in her mother's house for some time after her first child is born, in fact until her husband has built her a woman's house in his kepūn area, but her social status is that of a married woman and she now wears a waist cloth, and not the narrow fibre girdle of a young girl or a bride.

Marital status of women was also marked until recently by chipping and blackening the incisor teeth. This mutilation should properly be

carried out towards the end of the seclusion period by Omengka a member
of the priests' council (Yabot) who performs this operation for women on
marriage and also for the priests themselves on installation.   From the
father of all brides Omengka is entitled to a payment of two shillings for
operating, but there has in practice been much evasion and the operation
has been carried out without fee or for a smaller sum by women of   no
status. If illicit tooth chipping came to his notice Omengka could demand a payment from the parents but in practice this was rarely done in
recent years in Umor, partly, no doubt, because the community was so large
and marriages so frequent that one operator could barely have met the demand, while the notion that the Omengka should become a full time specialist depending entirely on the proceeds of this operation was quite foreign
to the Yako. Chipped teeth, although the operation itself is carried out
without accompanying ceremony, is a ritual mark of the status of a married
woman not a variety of beauty specialism. After chipping, women, like the
priests of matrilineal clans, habitually use lengths of a dried root (etūn)
as chew sticks which blacken their teeth.

But during the past ten or fifteen years there has been a revolt a-
gainst tooth chipping on the part of both young women and their husbands.
This has been stimulated by more frequent contacts with other peoples who
do not practice this mutilation and by the indirect infiltration of European standards through young men's visits to Calabar and other big trading centres. Thus while almost all women of age sets XIV and older in Umor
have chipped teeth it is exceptional to find a young married women of sets
XVII and XVIII who has.

Throughout the foregoing account of marriage ceremonials we have been
concerned with the first marriage of a young girl, or more precisely with
the passage of a female from the status of girl (mōna) to that of married
woman (yanen). Marital status is in the ceremonial sense irrevocable. A
woman may be widowed or divorced but she does not revert to the status of
a girl and any subsequent marital relation into which she may enter into
does not involve repetition of these rites. There is no betrothal obligation to the parents of a widow or divorcee and no firewood rite, wedding
feast or seclusion takes place. For a widow or divorcee marital status is
re-established simply by the assumption of residence with the new spouse
and the adjustment of the position with regard to marriage payment.

CHAPTER VII

RITES DURING THE FIRST PREGNANCY

When a bride becomes pregnant, or, if likpŏkot was performed, soon after the clitorodectomy wound is healed, further rituals are performed with the avowed purpose of ensuring a safe and successful birth.

Patriclan rite of "Putting the Navel". The first of these known as lekŏ kegen (= navel putting), takes place at the shrine (epŭndet) of the bride's patriclan to which her father takes her and it is performed by the priest-head (Obot Kepŭn). The bride's father brings the supplies needed for the rite. These should consist of two legs of smoked meat (antelope and duiker), a live chicken, four calabashes of wine, two large bowls of fufu, four sticks of chalk, a pot of water from a particular spring in the village known as Yibŏ, and some palm oil in a calabash. All these are placed on the ground in front of the clan shrine while the head, his assistant and a few clan elders squat on the stones. Other men of the clan of all ages sit in the adjacent assembly house to watch the ritual and join in the subsequent feast. The bride wears only a bark cloth strip held between the legs by a waist string but her closest age set friend, the only other woman to take part, carries a waist cloth which the bride puts on and wears for the first time after the rite. The Obot Kepŭn tells the bride to lie flat on her back before the shrine. He cuts four small pieces of the bush meat and taking two of them, one in each hand, dips them in the palm oil, touches the girl's jaw on either side and finally throws them on the shrine. He repeats this with the other two pieces of meat. His assistant now grasps the chicken and holds it over the front stones of the shrine while the priest beheads it with a matchet. The blood is allowed to drip on to the stones and some feathers plucked from the body are dropped on the splashes of blood. The carcase is then put on one side to be cooked and eaten by the priest and elders and the father of the bride later in the morning after the ceremony. The priest now pours a few drops of water from the jar of Libŏ spring water on to the chalk mixing stone of the shrine and another on the belly of the bride. This is done four times in all and on the last occasion all the remaining water is poured over the bride's belly. He now makes paste of chalk on the mixing stone with one of the sticks, presses his hands in this and then smears them diagonally across the chest of the bride. He offers her his hands to help her to rise, and the bride extends her own hands cupped together first to the priest himself and then to the clan elders seated round the shrine. Each in turn breathes on them, the Yakŏ symbol of welfare, and the priest then tells her to go to her home in peace. No verbal appeal is addressed to the shrine throughout the rite and once the girl has departed the atmosphere changes to that of cheerful feasting. The wine is poured into pots and the food is eaten.

This rite is clearly intended, and is regarded by the Yakŏ as intend-

40

ing, to ensure the blessing of the patriclan spirit on the bride as a clan member about to bear her first child. It is to be observed, however, that the child will not be a member of that patriclan while no similar rite is performed at the shrine of the groom to whose patriclan the child when born will, by the rule of patrilineal affiliation, belong.

Rite at the Fertility Shrine of the Bride's Matriclan. A similar but less elaborate rite is performed at the shrine of the matriclan of the bride to which she is taken during her pregnancy by her mother and her mother's brother. They hand an offering, usually a chicken, a yam and some wine, to the priest (ina) of the yose who while beheading the chicken and pouring wine before the shrine prays for a safe and successful delivery and finally, as in all yose rituals, mixes a chalk paste which he smears on the bride and those who accompany her. If the bride is pregnant before marriage this rite will, as has been indicated, and unlike the lekö kegen rite, usually be performed before the marriage rite.

The Ketūkpoli Rite. The third rite, which is performed at the shrine of a spirit known as Ketūkpoli believed to influence the outcome of a first pregnancy, follows the leko kegen rite on the next ōpongōbi. There are two such shrines in Umor, one in Idjiman and the other in Ukpakapi ward, but their locations have no particular significance and the bride may go to either at choice. Each is in charge of a priestess known as Ma Ketūk-poli who must be a member of a particular matriclan (Yabōni for the Idji-man shrine, and Yabung for the Ukpakapi shrine) in whose house the para-phernalia are kept.

The bride's father, or her husband if he wishes and knows the procedure, goes out in the early morning to his palm tapping ground and brings back a wine collecting calabash with a little wine in it and a bunch of leaves known as litūkpoliwa on account of their use in this rite. From the firewood stack in the bride's compound he takes a pole of dead koweli wood some seven feet long and binds to one end of it eight smaller sticks of koweli. This he gives to the bride to carry on her head to the house of Ma Ketūkpoli while he, assisted by a small boy or two, brings the collecting calabash, a calabash full of wine, the bundle of leaves, a water yam (ōbulö), a bowl of palm oil and a bowl of pounded black dye (eblōmi) root. The bride wears a bark cloth strip held by a girdle of undyed raphia fibre. Ma Ketupoli places on the bride's left ankle and right arm two fibre rings which she wears throughout the rite. She then peels the yam and shreds part of it on to a few of the leaves while the bride chops the koweli wood with a matchet and takes it into the house to be put on the fire. The shredded yam wrapped in leaves is put on to boil and Ma Ketūkpoli goes into an inner cubicle containing the shrine to invoke the spirit for a painless and successful childbirth. The words of the invocation are not heard by the bride or her father. All three eat the boiled yam and leaves mixed with oil and drink some of the wine. Ma Ketūkpoli repeatedly asks the bride

and her father how much they want of the food and gives them the opposite.
They know that she will do this and reply accordingly.   This is the only
instance of inverted speech which I encountered among the Yakö.

   Ma Ketūkpoli next prepares dye paint by squeezing the eblömi root into a little water in which it has been soaking and mixing in powdered charcoal.   She shaves the bride's head and then proceeds to paint circular bands
of black paint round the arm and leg joints, the buttocks, the belly,   the
small of the back, the neck, the forehead and the top of the head. She then
produces bowls of powdered red camwood (ekö), white chalk and yellow   wood
powder (edjünga). Mixing some of each separately with water she dabs spots
of each colour inside the paint rings.   Decorated in this highly coloured
way the bride returns to her house; no notice should be taken of her by
bystanders as she walks through the village nor should any audible comment
on her appearance be made.   Once home again she must remain in her seclusion cubicle until the next kokö when she goes with one or two of her friends
to the bathing pool and removes the paint.

CHAPTER VIII

THE FREQUENCY OF PRE-MARITAL PREGNANCY

The kekpopam rite performed before pregnancy, is regarded as the standard and desirable preliminary to marriage and betrothed girls are frequently urged by their mothers to avoid intercourse in order that they may have kekpopam. Parents have direct personal preference since, as has been seen, the marriage ceremonies are more elaborate, and so redound to their prestige, while the gifts that they then receive are more substantial than after likpŏkōt.

Nevertheless, kekpopam occurs in a minority of cases at the present day, for the great majority of girls are pregnant before clitorodectomy and the wedding feasts take place. In order to determine conditions in the recent past and any trends that might exist an investigation of the clitorodectomy rites performed for 288 wives of men of one patriclan in Umor was undertaken. The age set memberships of these women were known, and the enquiry reveals that there has been a considerable change during the past fifty years in the proportion of girls who were pregnant at the time of their first marriage.

From Table 1 it may be seen that among the 26 old women of age-sets I-V (aged approximately 60 years and over in 1939) only half were pregnant at the time of their clitoridectomy. About the same proportions hold for the 42 women of sets VI-IX (approximately 60 to 48 years) and the 47 women of sets X-XI (48 to 40 years) i.e. 50 and 45% respectively. But of the 59 women of sets XII-XIII (approximately 48 to 30 years and the 52 women of sets XIV-XV (approximately 30 to 24 years) only a third (31 and 33% respectively) had the kekpopam rite while among the youngest women of sets XVI-XVIII (approximately 17 to 24 years) the proportion has fallen sharply to about one sixth (16%). It is clear that in the period from the 1870s down to the second decade of this century premarital intercourse was sufficiently general to result in pregnancy before marriage in about half the instances. Since that time, however, there has been a sharp increase in the incidence of pregnancy before the clitoridectomy rite is held, with the result that the orthodox marriage procedure is generally honoured in the breach.[1] This change is no doubt due to a number of factors, the relative force of which

---

[1] The increase is probably greater than these figures suggest for in the earlier period more foreign female children were purchased for adoption than during the past twenty years and at that time kekpopam could not be performed for these adopted girls while in more recent times this discrimination has been dropped.

TABLE 1 Relative frequency by Age Sets of Clitoridectomy before and during pregnancy among 288 wives of Ndai men

	I	II	III	IV	V	VI	VII	VIII	IX	X	XI	XII	XIII	XIV	XV	XVI	XVII	XVIII	Rite
K	–	1	1	4	7	10	3	5	3	16	8	9	7	6	11	7	3	–	Kekpɔpam 101 = 35%
L	–	1	–	5	7	7	4	7	4	11	16	19	24	8	27	25	18	4	Lîîkpökôt 187 = 65%

Group (Age Grades)	I–V	VI–IX	X–XI	XII–XIII	XIV–XV	XVI–XVIII	Total
Sub-total	26	43	51	59	52	57	Total K + L = 288 = 100%
K	K – 13 = 50%	21 = 48·8%	24 = 47·1%	16 = 27·1%	17 = 32·7%	10 = 17·5%–K	
L	L – 13 = 50%	22 = 51·2%	27 = 52·9%	43 = 72·9%	35 = 67·3%	47 = 82·5%–L	
Approx. age range 1939	80 – 60 yrs.	60 – 48 yrs.	48 – 40 yrs.	40–30 yrs.	30–24 yrs.	24 – 17 yrs.	
Approx. time range	1876 – 1896	1896 – 1908	1908–1916	1916–26	1926–32	1932 – 1939	

K. = Kekpɔpam i.e. before pregnancy

L = Lîîkpökôt i.e. during pregnancy

it was not possible to determine. Among these are fluctuations in economic
prosperity associated with the development of an external market. There are
indications that in recent times the level of marriage payments has not res-
ponded immediately to declines in palm product prices with a result that a
lack of available currency has induced youths and their parents to delay their
undertaking to marry and make the marriage payment asked. Since, among the
Yako, the period of betrothal is not of definite length and permits sexual
intimacy between the youth and his intended bride any extension of the period
will increase the likelihood of pregnancy. These considerations depend,
however, on another change for which there is evidence in the statements and
attitudes of informants of different ages, namely that completed coitus
between unmarried lovers is more frequent today than in the past.

CHAPTER IX

MARRIAGE MONEY : LIBEMAN

We may now turn to a consideration of the transfer at marriage of property which the Yakö themselves term 'marriage money' (libeman).It has been
seen that at a well ordered first marriage of a woman the marriage money is
handed over by the groom's age mates to those of the bride who immediately
transfer it to her father. But that is by no means the end of the matter.
Matrilineal kin of the bride have customary rights and obligations in connection with this transfer. After the last wedding feast given by the bride's
parents to their friends the father should go, or send a message to, the
closest senior male among the matrilineal relatives of the bride,one who is
her 'mother's brother', informing him that the wedding feasts have been concluded, that the marriage payment has been made and that he is ready to hand
over the customary portion to him. The 'mother's brother' with one or two
more of the matrilineal relatives will come on the next kokö to the father's
compound where some of his age mates will be present as witnesses.The father
offers palm wine, the bride is saluted and, after discussion concerning the
amount to be handed over, the transfer should be made.

In recent years in Umor the traditional rights and obligations with regard to the mother's brother's share of the marriage money have been under-
mined. There is general agreement as to traditional rights but these are
being increasingly repudiated by fathers and when repudiated are no longer
enforced. By custom the father should hand over to the 'mother's brother'
the greater part of the payment. By so doing, however, he is absolved from
any responsibility to his son-in-law for the return of the payment. The
bridegroom and his relatives can make no claim on him should the wife desert
her husband. All such responsibility is transferred with the transferred
portion of the marriage money to the mother's brother. The proportion handed over in such circumstances will range from four-fifths to two-thirds of
the amount provided by or on behalf of the husband. The remainder which the
father keeps involves him in no liability. On the other hand the liability
of the mother's brother may, as will be seen, be heavy for it is his legal
obligation to compensate the husband if the wife deserts him, or his patrilineal kin if as a widow she remarries within a year or two of his death.
The mother's brother can in turn claim a marriage payment from the new spouse
of a widow or divorcee.

Underlying all this are the Yakö principles of matrilineal kinship obligations. Transferable wealth is inherited by matrilineal relatives, a
man's goods, his yams, his livestock, his money and household property,
all pass into the control of a close matrilineal kinsmen,usually a sister's
son at his death; loans to a matrilineal relative cannot be recovered by action at law, responsibility for a bankrupt's debts rests on his matrilineal

kin.[1] The obligation of a woman to serve her husband dutifully is regarded in the same way. If she fails it is the duty of her matrilineal kin in the person of the mother's brother to restore an appropriate part of the marriage money handed over by the husband. It is in virtue of this obligation that matrilineal kin claim that a substantial portion should be transferred to them. Fathers have, however, in recent times been reluctant to make this transfer and have, when challenged, declared that they would themselves assume the responsibility of meeting claims for return of marriage money. I was told in Umor that several cases of this kind came before the Yabot(= the Leaders), the indigenous village council[2] during the past twenty years and that it had become customary to decide that the father might make only a token payment to the matrilineal kinsman of the bride and be declared to have sole responsibility for the return of marriage money. I did not learn that token payments in actual money, as distinct from an offering of a calabash of wine, have usually been made in such cases, but the principle that the father may retain the marriage money and therewith the responsibility for its return to the husband or his successors in certain circumstances is now generally recognised.

I was, however, frequently told that this was usually done only by rich men (yasū, sing. osū). This may at first sight seem surprising, since to them the amount involved might appear to be of little moment, while motives of cupidity would be stronger on the part of a poor father. But two distinct conditions operate to limit the practice in this sense. In the first place a mother's brother can rely on his matrilineal kinsmen to assist him in providing the means of returning a marriage payment, but a father cannot do this. The marriage is not the close concern of the father's matrilineal kin, his daughter is not to them a wenwa wenamūka(=sister's child) and does not belong to their matrilineal lineage (kejimafat). Nor can the father reasonably turn to his patrilineal kin since the daughter's children do not belong to their patrilineage (epōnama). Thus a father who retains the marriage payment faces the possibility of having to return a large part of it, perhaps many years later, entirely from his own resources. This risk a poor man would be reluctant to assume.

Furthermore, a man of means among the Yakö, one who has many dependent helpers, a large farm and a hoard of currency takes pride in his wealth and it is customary to display it. Until recent years he would have bought foreign children (yafoli) whom he adopted into both his patrilineal and his

---

[1] See Forde, Kinship in Umor, Amer. Anthropologist, 41,1939,536 ff.

[2] See Forde, Government in Umor, Africa, 12,1939, 136.

matrilineal lineages. With the increasing curtailment of this practice under Government penalties the opportunity to display his means by freely taking responsibility for the marriages of his daughters appears to have become increasingly attractive. In any case ostentation was clearly a considerable motive behind several of the cases which I investigated of refusal to transfer marriage payment to the mother's brother. In an instance of
which I learned most of the circumstances a ward head in Umor who was also
prominent in the premier men's secret society refused in the early twenties
to hand over the marriage payment for his daughter to the priest of her matrilineal clan who was her closest senior matrilineal relative.The marriage
payment of £6. 5. 0 was brought to his compound on the day of the likpokot
rite and the father made his daughter's age set friends a customary gift of
5/-. On the koko following the marriage feasts the ina of Atalikumi, priest
of the Yabaye lejima to which the bride belonged, came to the father saying
that he had learned that his daughter's husband had made the full marriage
payment and that he now claimed the customary portion as the bride's closest
matrilineal kinsman. The ward head replied that the marriage payment should
not be divided, he would keep it all safely himself and if his daughter should
leave her husband he would make any payment without asking any help from her
matrilineal kin. The priest expostulated and the father admitted that it
was right by custom to hand over the greater part to a matrilineal kinsman
but that he was too big a man to do this. He would follow the new way for
he could return the marriage payment of his daughter many times over. The
priest was very angry and finally warned the father that if he persisted in
the breach of custom his daughter's child would sicken and die.This was regarded as a threat on the part of the priest who might be expected to invoke the supernatural power of the fertility spirit (yose) Atalikumi, but
the father would not give way. The child when born was sickly and as it
grew worse the husband protested vehemently to his father-in-law that the
life of the child, which belonged to his kepun and not to that of the father-
in-law, was being endangered by the refusal to recognise the rights of his
wife's matrilineal kin. He was supported by the head of his kepun and several older men of his lineage. After the dispute and the child's sickness
had been widely talked of and it was clear that he and not the priest was
generally regarded as the real offender, the wife's father finally gave way.
He went with the husband to the priest taking the entire marriage payment
saying: 'I know you are harming the child because you have not had your
portion of the marriage payment. Now you can take the whole of it. I have
been keeping it to save you trouble for I am a rich man (osu) and can look
after my own daughters.' To offer the entire payment was ostentatious and
contemptuous. The priest replied by denying that he had invoked the spirit
of his clan to harm the child which of course belonged to the same lejima.
He claimed that when the father-in-law had refused to abide by custom he had
put the dispute out of his mind and insisted that he would no longer accept
the payment or have any concern with the marriage. The husband who was still
anxious both for the child's health interceded and begged him to end the
quarrel and restore the child's health. Finally the priest accepted 4/- as

a token payment to indicate that he bore no ill will to his sister's daughter and her child, but he refused to accept his full share or any responsibility for later repayment of the marriage money. The husband who gave me details of this dispute himself added that both the priest and everybody else knew quite well that the ward head was indeed a rich man and much better able to meet any claim for repayment than the priest who would probably dissipate it and find difficulty in meeting any claim later on.

In order to discover the frequency with which this and other new practices had occurred in recent years I investigated the circumstances of the first marriages of a sample of Yakö women of various ages who had married men of one patrilineal kin group. On this particular point I could not obtain satisfactory data for women who were more than about forty years of age in 1939 i.e. women of age-sets X and senior, while data for the youngest women, i.e. those of the most junior set, XVIII (aged from approximately 15 to 18 years in 1939) was scanty as many girls of that set were still unmarried.

TABLE 2   Incidence of transfers of marriage money to matrilineal kin at 157
first marriages of women to Ndai men

Age Sets of Wives.	None received from father by matrilineal relative.	Portion handed over by father to matrilineal relative.	All received direct from groom by matrilineal relative.	Total.
XI	7	6	6	19
XII	3	11	4	18
XIII	8	10	5	23
XIV	1	4	3	8
XV	9	10	11	30
XVI	11	10	12	33
XVII	14	6	6	26
	53	57	47	157
		= 36·3%	= 29·9%	

104
66·2%

= 33·8%   100%

As will be seen in Table 2, among 157 women of age-sets XI to XVII inclusive i.e. women of between approximately forty and eighteen years of age in 1939, first married during the previous 26 years, there were 53 instances, or 34% in which the father, or someone acting in his place other than a matrilineal relative of the bride, received the marriage payment but transferred none of it to a matrilineal kinsman of the bride. In 57 cases or 36% of this sample the marriage payment was received by the father and the major part handed over to the mother's brother while in 47 cases or 30% the payment was received by a matrilineal relative directly from the bridegroom. The different sets when considered separately showed apart from the most junior no substantial variation among themselves so that the incidence of retention of the marriage payment by the father, which amounts to nearly half the cases in which the payment was received by the father, seems to have been fairly steady during the past quarter of a century. On the other hand the small sample of married women of age-set XVIII, only 11 in number, showed a much higher incidence, 9 cases, or a rate of 81%, of retention of the payment by the father. This may be the chance of a small sample, but there are indications in the data for set XVII as well as in the views of the people themselves that a marked increase in the practice was setting in during the period of my field work and that this was connected with a general strain which increasing individualism and the depression of the external market for palm products were imposing on the whole system of marriage payments. This wider issue will be considered later.

TABLE 3 Relatives of Bride receiving Marriage Payment from Bridegroom at First Marriages of 157 Women of Sets XI-XVII to Ndai Men

Age Set of Bride	Father	Full Brother	Mother's Brother	Paternal Half Brother	Step-Father	Total
XI	12	7	–	–	–	19
XII	13	4	1	–	–	18
XIII	16	5	2	–	–	23
XIV	5	3	–	–	–	8
XV	18	11	1	–	–	30
XVI	19	11	2	1	–	33
XVII	16	6	–	1	3	26
	99	47	6	2	3	157
	63·1%	29·9%	3·8%	1·3%	1·9%	100%

It was assumed earlier that the father always received the marriage payment but it is obvious that in a disrupted family another recipient may be involved. If the father is unable, owing to death or migration, or unwilling to play his part in the marriage of his daughter the person considered most appropriate is a full brother of the bride of mature years. In the sample of 157 women referred to above the marriage payment was received by the bride's father in only 99 cases or 63%. Details for the several age-sets are indicated in Table 3. In 47 or 30% of the cases it was received not by the father but by a full brother. When a senior full brother acts in this way the further transfer of a portion to a matrilineal kinsman does not arise, for the full brother is himself one of the closest matrilineal kinsman of the bride and can assume the status of a mother's brother as well as that of the father. Failing the father and in the absence of a fully adult full brother the bride's mother's brother will often seek to receive the libeman direct from the groom, especially if the mother has as occasionally happens joined his household, but there were only six cases or 4% in this sample. Others who occasionally act in place of the father are the paternal half-brother, of which there were only two instances in the sample referred to above, and the step-father, of which there were only three instances all very recent. The former is of course a close patrilineal kinsman of the bride and thereby a justifiable substitute of the father. The step-father, or ūwo keplakū (= daylight father) in the Yako idiom, is of course not a kinsman of the bride and can act in this way only by virtue of his dominance in the household in which she may have been brought up. The last five cases were included among the 'fathers' in the earlier classification, while the full brothers were counted as 'mother's brothers'.

The source of the marriage money. It has been seen that the marriage money should be taken to the bride's father by the age mates of the groom on or before the day of the clitorodectomy rite. For this to be done the full amount should be available on that day; but the amassing of the marriage money will have been a matter of concern for the groom and his near kin long before this. If the groom is a youth who is marrying for the first time, or even a young man taking a second wife, he will usually be quite unable to provide the amount himself. Traditionally a youth relies on his father to provide the libeman at his first marriage, but he or the father may also seek contributions from his other close kinsmen and particularly the groom's older brothers and his 'mother's brothers'. If he has care of the groom and is thus his foster-father the mother's brother replaces the father as the main contributor, but otherwise he is expected to make only a small gift. From Table 4 it will be seen that in 84 first marriages of Ndai men to women of age-sets XI to XVII i.e. women between 40 and 18 years old in 1939, while small amounts may have been, and probably were, contributed by such kinsfolk as the older brothers, mothers, father's brothers and mother's brothers of the groom, the marriage money was substantially provided by the groom's father in 42, or 49%, of the cases. Full or paternal half brothers were the second largest class of relatives who were the main providers of marriage payments, accounting for 25, or 28%, of the cases or little more than half as frequently as the father. The duty of a senior patrilineal brother to undertake the responsibilities of a deceased father in respect of younger brothers is well established among the Yako and deaths of fathers before the marriage of their younger sons probably accounts for the high proportion of cases in which a brother of the groom acts in the father's place.

Only one instance occurred of a father's brother being the main provider of libeman and this is in accord with general custom that senior brothers of the groom, not father's brothers, have first responsibility in this respect. There were only three instances in which the mother's brother and two in which a step-father was the main provider. The groom himself provided the greater part himself more frequently than any relatives except fathers and older brothers. There were 12, or 14%, of these cases which occurred in all but the most senior of the women's age-sets involved. In recent years petty trading, road making and other activities open to a minority of young men who are prepared to leave the village at intervals make it possible to accumulate currency to make their own marriage payments. In the past before such opportunities existed payment by the groom was probably rarer but even then a young man might inherit property from a deceased mother's brother early enough to make his own payment for his first marriage.

TABLE 4. Main Providers of Marriage Money at 84 First Marriages of Ndai Men to Young Girls by Age Sets of Brides

Age Set of Bride	Father	Groom	Full Brother	Paternal Half Brother	Mother's Brother	Step Father	Father's Brother	Total
XI	5		1	3				9
XII	8	2	1	1				12
XIII	3	3		5	1	1		13
XIV	2			1		1		4
XV	11	3	1	4	1			20
XVI	9	1	1	1				12
XVII	3	3	2	4	1		1	14
Sets XI-XVII inclusive	41	12	6	19	3	2	1	84
=	48·9%	14·2%	7·1%	22·6%	3·6%	2·4%	1·2%	100%

But although the father or a patrilineal brother,who is the father's customary successor in this obligation, is in the great majority of cases (79% in this sample) the main provider of the libeman there is a kinship obligation on all close adult relatives of the groom to make a contribution in case of need. At the present time a few shillings are sought from senior brothers, mother's brothers, father's brothers and also from the mother and her sisters. It is to be observed that these relatives fall into two classes: the patrilineal kinsmen who belong to a lineage and clan for which the groom may be expected to beget children, and the matrilineal relatives to none of whose descent groups patrilineal or matrilineal will the children of the groom belong. But, apart from the father (actual or substitute) who has the prime responsibility, I could not determine any clear cut difference in obligation or attitude among them. A father if he is a man of substance usually takes pride in making the entire payment himself; but if he cannot, or is unwilling to do so, he will tell his son that he should seek the aid of his close senior relatives. The patrilineal relatives will usually be neighbours and intimates of the father, who already know from him of the desire for gifts. His mother's brothers and occasionally her sisters are on the other hand living elsewhere not in daily contact with the household of the bridegroom who must approach them himself. He may have his mother's support, but his father does not solicit their aid. Any contributions of these relatives matrilineal or patrilineal are regarded as free gifts to the groom or his father. They may create the expectation of later reciprocal gifts on similar occasions from the father or the groom but they do not give the relatives a claim to a share in the marriage payment should it be returned if the marriage is later dissolved.

As has been indicated above a young man can, if his father, fosterfather or father's brothers have the means, obtain their support in providing the greater part of the amount of further marriage payments for later wives. But by the time a man has reached early maturity,at 30 years or so, he, as a rule, will be expected to provide the greater part himself. In discussing marriage money with Yakö it became very clear that, apart from the recent difficulties in maintaining former scales of payment, the obligation on the part of the father to provide the means for the groom's marriage is one which is as a rule cheerfully and even proudly accepted. The cyclic character of the process is consciously recognised. I have been told: "My father gave my marriage money and I will do so for my sons and they too will grow up and give for my grandsons to marry."

The Nature of 'Bride Wealth' among the Yakö. The essential character of the marriage payment and its relation to other Yakö social institutions may now be considered. It is clearly a variety of the institution of 'bride wealth' commonly found in African societies and, while no far reaching comparisons with other forms can be undertaken here, it is pertinent to consider its characteristics in relation to those which have been claimed for

'bride wealth' elsewhere. The Yako 'marriage money' is substantially provided by one person, the father of the groom or the groom himself. But it
is transferred by the age mates of the groom on his behalf and not by, or on
behalf of, his father. It is received in the first place by the father of
the bride during the series of ceremonial acts by which the status of the
bride as a married woman is established and the transference is itself one
of those acts. The greater part of the marriage money should later be
handed over, in the presence of witnesses but without ceremonial observance,
by the bride's father to her mother's brother who thereby assumes responsibility for returning the entire amount or an appropriate portion of it if
the marriage is dissolved through fault of the wife.

Any assistance in making the payment that may be given to the groom or
his father **on this occasion are acts** of generosity to a kinsman, They
depend on the circumstances of the persons concerned and cannot be regarded as specific obligations. It is moreover to be noted that, relative to
the wife's father and mother's brother, the marriage money is to be regarded as provided by the husband. It is he, not his father or any other kinsman, who can claim its return and the fact that it is the groom himself who
offers it is emphasised in the transfer. The age mates of the groom, not
his father or any of the father's kinsmen or friends, bring it to the bride's
compound and the groom's father is not present at the transfer.

While the mother's brother of the bride is not expected to distribute
the marriage money he receives among his relatives matrilineal or patrilineal there is an obligation on his close matrilineal kin to assist him
if necessary should the return of the payment to the groom become necessary. This obligation is however not peculiar to the marriage payment. It
is but an instance of a general principle recognised in Yakö law that rights
in and obligations concerning moveable property pass to matrilineal kin.

It is to be observed in the first place that there is no symmetry or
direct reciprocity in marriage payments. A father providing for his son
does not receive for his daughter or, more precisely, he receives on a much
smaller scale for his daughter than he gives for his son. A mother's brother receiving for a bride does not give correspondingly for her brothers.
He gives for his own son. The unorthodox procedure whereby a father usurps
the rights and obligations of the mother's brother does however establish
a potential symmetry in this respect although actual symmetry is likely to
be exceptional even then since few men will have marriageable sons and
daughters in equal numbers. Nor is there symmetry in the social groups involved; the provider may not be a group but the father or the groom alone,
but if other kinsmen contribute they are likely to include both patrilineal
and matrilineal relatives of the groom who are linked together only by their
several interests in the welfare of the groom. The groom's patrilineage
and clan have no corporate concern in the transfer or in its future resti-
tution. Nor does the mother's brother receive the marriage payment as a

representative of the bride's patrilineal or matrilineal lineages or clans. He receives it personally as a matrilineal relative.

The father and the mother's brother of the bride, who share the marriage money, are affinal relatives but they receive it in virtue of their kinship with the bride and the relations to the husband which this entails do not conform with Dr. Evans Pritchard's suggestion that "it is the relation between a man and his brothers or wife's brothers that is being expressed (in bride wealth distribution). The distribution is generally, and I think erroneously, treated as though it were primarily a recognition of the relationship between a girl and her patrilineal and matrilineal uncles."[1] Among the Yakö it clearly is because he is the bride's maternal uncle not because he is her father's brother-in-law that the mother's brother receives the greater portion of the marriage payment.

Since the marriage payment is not mainly retained by the father it can not be considered, and is not regarded by the Yakö, as primarily an indemnity for the loss of the girl when she leaves her father's household and the dwelling area of his patriclan.[2] Nor is it an indemnity to the mother's brother who, far from suffering any loss, expects her to bear his heirs and might on the contrary be expected to owe an obligation to her husband for enabling her to bear and rear them.

There is again no indication that it is regarded, or actually operates, among the Yakö in the manner further suggested by Evans Pritchard as a "mechanism of effecting exchange of women between exogamous groups alternative to and more flexible than wife exchange or preferential mating"; for the "principle of equivalence - in return for a wife you receive a wife"[3] which it is claimed underlies bride wealth is here conspicuously absent. Among the Yakö in return for marriage money the giver or his son receives the services of a wife and rights of custody and paternity over her children. In return for receiving marriage money and the expectation of heirs a Yakö recognises the relationship and assumes the obligation to refund the money if his sister's daughter fails through her fault to perform those services satisfactorily.

The Yakö marriage payment unlike some East African forms of 'bride-wealth' is not continued over a long period. It should be transferred complete when the marriage is established and returned complete, or in such proportion as is appropriate, when the marriage is dissolved through default of the wife. No further payments during the period of marriage, as

---

[1] Evans Pritchard, E.E.   Man. 1934, 194, p.174.

[2] Radcliffe Brown, A.R.   Man. 1929, 96.

[3] Evans Pritchard, E.E.   Op.cit., p.175.

for instance at the birth of children, are expected. On the other hand the proportion returnable on dissolution is made dependent on the duration and fertility of the union. The death of either spouse terminates the liability of the wife's matrilineal kin.

There is no doubt that it is the transfer of the libeman which gives the husband legal rights to his wife's services and to the social father-hood of the children born to her during the marriage. Conversely if a man had handed over none or only part of the marriage money by the time that his wife comes to live with him and continues to defer the payment while refusing to allow the woman to depart, an order may be obtained from the Native Court requiring the return of the woman to the custody of her father or of a matrilineal kinsman. The court records at Umor include several instances of such orders being sought and obtained by fathers or by matrilineal kinsmen. Before the establishment and general resort of the Yakö to the Native Courts such claims of kinsmen were heard and, if established, enforced by either the ward heads or the village councils.

The retention by the bride's father of a portion of the marriage money, which entails no future obligations on his part, establishes his recognition of the marriage and his consent to the bride's departure from his household; but here again it is to be doubted whether it had the character of an indemnity. Although a Yakö father undoubtedly regards this share of the marriage money as a right, and might say that it was due to him because he had reared the bride from childhood - although this is in fact by no means always the actual case - he cannot be considered to suffer loss since there is no expectation of economic or other benefits from a daughter that are frustrated by marriage.

The retention of a portion of the marriage money by the father, like its initial transfer by the groom to him, is to be accounted for not by any economic value of a daughter, nor by compensation for loss of the presence in his household of a loved child. It is to be explained by the fact of paternal authority in the household. A father has established right to control the domicile of his unmarried children. No daughter may legally go or be removed from his household and parental authority without his consent. The acceptance of the marriage money and the retention of a portion of it marks the termination of the father's parental authority and places him under a legal obligation to consent to his daughter's departure from his household. His share of the marriage payment is a con-sideration for that consent.

But the husband is securing at marriage not merely the curtailment of paternal authority over the bride. He is also placing the bride under obligation to perform certain services. Should she fail compensation can-not be secured from the bride herself and the obligation to return the marriage money to the husband devolves not on the father but on those who in

Yako" law have responsibility for ensuring the fulfilment or compensation of all personal obligations namely the matrilineal kin. It is on account of this potential obligation that a matrilineal kinsman is consideredentitled to claim from the father the greater part of the payment.It should be observed that this obligation covers the whole of the marriage money including the portion retained by the father. It is not an obligation to return what was received but a total obligation in respect of the payment made by the husband. That the kinsman to undertake it and to receive the greater part of the marriage money in consideration should be the mother's brother is consonant with the Yako" principle of matrilineal transmission. As the closest matrilineal kinsman senior in generation to the wife compensation would be claimed from him if she should fail in her marital obligations, while her matrilineal brothers are successors to both this obligation and to the property of the mother's brother.

Thus Yako"'bride wealth' cannot be said to have a single value or social function. This transfer of property takes place in a complex social context and is variously related to the several interests involved. It expresses the value of a wife to her husband and ensures his intention to maintain a stable union. It rewards the bride's father for the renunciation of his parental authority while establishing his consent and that of the matrilineal kin to the acquisition of marital rights by the husband. It reinforces the responsibility of matrilineal kin for ensuring that the wife shall fulfil her marital obligations by giving the closest senior matrilineal kinsman of the bride a pecuniary responsibility for her good conduct.

When there is no subsequent transfer of marriage money from the father to the mother's brother of the bride recognition of the husband's marital rights is confined to the father, and it is accepted that the matrilineal kin of the wife have no obligation to compensate the husband for defection on her part. Contrary to the general Yako" principle of the exclusive responsibility of matrilineal kinsfolk for personal delinquence, the responsibility of the father for the good conduct of the wife in such circumstances has been established.

<u>Changes in the Amounts of Marriage Money.</u> Marriage payments have always, so far as Yako" memory extends, always been made mainly in   currency although in earlier days when game was more abundant and hunting more active smoked bush meat which the bride's father used for the wedding feats could be substituted for currency. Older men mentioned smoked legs of antelope to the number of from ten to twenty as being customary. These converted at a standard rate, offset a corresponding amount of rod currency. One account referred to two or more entire antelope carcases, valued at 30 rods each, bundles of split creeper for farm and harvest stack tying, valued at 3 rods each and 40 calabashes of wine valued at 20 rods as frequent items in the payment. But the practice of making

part of the marriage payment in food supplies and other goods has now disappeared. For the last 20 years or so marriage payments in Umor at least have nearly always been made in Nigerian coinage, before that brass rods were used as far as my records of actual payments extend, although it was sometimes claimed that in a more remote past the 'hoe money'(nkase), which is used today only ceremonially, was a medium of payment.

I endeavoured to obtain data on the amounts of the payments at the marriages of the oldest living women, but for age sets prior to VIII i.e. for women 55 years old and over in 1939, i.e. likely to have been first married forty or more years ago, statements were so uniform that I suspect that a standard amount, rather than the actual payment, was frequently given. This standard amount was 440 rods. Payments stated to have been made at the first marriage of eleven women of age sets VIII & IX (c.48 to 55 years old in 1939) and likely to have been first married between thirty to forty years ago ranged from 440 to 240 rods, nine of them being at the higher figure. Among the sample of seventeen women of set X, likely to have been first married between 32 and 26 years ago, full payment of 440 rods were asserted in seven instances, in five cases only half this amount was paid while three others payments were said to have been made in Nigerian currency consisting of six guineas in two cases and five in the third. For the women of the next junior set (XI) first married between approximately 22 and 26 years ago, i.e. around 1915, payment in Nigerian currency was general. In only four of the nineteen cases was payment made in rods of amounts ranging from 440 to 420, while all the rest were in currency, 9 of six guineas and 2 of five guineas. From that time five to six guineas remained the standard amount of marriage money expected for nearly two decades. But the payments actually made were considerably less in a minority of cases at the marriages of women of sets XIII-XV (married between 8 and 24 years ago) while after those of set XVI the amounts demanded by the bride's parents declined in many cases to between £3. 15.0 and £1.10.0 while it was rare for more than £3 to be handed over. During the eight years immediately before 1939 payments occasionally fell as low as £1 or 10/- and while £5.5.0 has still been regarded as the proper amount for a marriage payment it was demanded in only a minority of the thirty seven marriages recorded and only quite exceptionally handed over. Thus among twenty nine women of set XVII first married during the previous six years, five guineas was asked as marriage payment in sixteen, but was actually paid in only seven instances. £2.10.0 or less was asked in thirteen cases and £1.10.0 or less was actually handed over in fourteen cases. Among eleven married women of set XVIII there is only one instance of five guineas being asked and paid.

The Yakö themselves attribute this recent decline in the amounts of marriage payments to a severe reduction in the amounts of currency in local circulation on account of the series of severe falls in the prices paid by the Cross River and Calabar factories for palm oil products. There is no doubt that the fluctuation of oil and kernel prices in recent years have resulted in a severe net decline. While palm oil production among the Yakö has been maintained and perhaps slightly increased during these years of depression the decline in prices has certainly not stimulated increased production sufficient to maintain the money incomes of twenty years ago. At the same time the demand for European trade goods has been maintained, and even increased. Cloths, matchets and enamel ware are indeed necessities today. The opportunities for accumulating currency have therefore been seriously curtailed in recent years. On the other hand the marked development of petty trading by men of the younger age sets in the last decade and the occasional opportunities for youths to work as labourers in Government service have given a small minority of young men more opportunities for accumulating currency than they would have had at earlier times. The increase of occasional trading activities among younger Yakö men who frequently visit, either on their own account or as servants of traders, the large coastal and interior markets of south-eastern Nigeria, and the speculative character of palm oil production have together with a decline in the solidarity of the clans and the authority of their priests and elders combined to encourage economic individualism in recent years. I gained the impression, which could unfortunately not be demonstrated by adequate case material, that the circle of mutual aid in economic affairs involving gifts of currency or produce had narrowed in recent times and that prosperous men were ready to use their wealth only for the benefit of their closest relatives.

The significance of the amount of marriage payment is of course relative to the wealth or rather the command over currency in the community as a whole. Statements by a number of men who had been producing palm products for a decade or more indicate that the more recent standard marriage payment of £5. 5. 0 was rather less than the return to which a man could, by the labour of his own household and dependents, obtain in one year by the sale of palm oil before the depression of prices in recent years. The kernels produced in such a household produced a further money income for the wife or wives, who among the Yakö have the customary right to sell them independently for their own benefit. Thus the estimates of pre-depression incomes from palm products in eight households of men with one or two wives ranged from £5 to £10 for oil and from £2.10. 0 to £5 for kernels. Recent annual incomes for palm products had in 1939 fallen to less than half of these figures.1 The relative value of the marriage

---

1 Factory prices at Umuahia in S.E.Nigeria,(with which the prices at Ediba on the Cross River seven miles from Umor and the chief local wholesale market for palm oil used by the Yakö - are known from comparisons made in 1935 and 1939 to correspond closely) per 4 gallon tin of semi-hard oil(the Yakö quality) ranged from 5/4d to 10½d in the period from April 1935 to March 1939, and was for most of this period around 2/6d per tin. In the early twenties semi-hard oil had fetched more than 10/- per 4 gallon tin over considerable periods.

payments may also be expressed in terms of yams the food staple of which considerable quantities are every year sold for export down river. Planting time prices for medium sized yams in Umor were in the years from 1935 to 1939 around 6/- per 100.[1] As the modal and mean harvests of Yakö farms, based on a sample of 97 farms investigated in 1935, were approximately 1900 and 2500 units of medium sized yams respectively and a considerable number of the larger farms yielded up to 5000 units of medium yams[2] it is clear that a marriage payment of £5.5.0 represents in terms of recent yam prices slightly less than the modal value and considerably less than the mean value of the annual yam harvests per farm namely approximately £5.14.0   and £7.10.0 respectively. It must however be borne in mind first that a harvest is the joint property of a man and one or more wives and secondly that a considerable part of it is required for replanting in the following year. Only a small part of the harvest of an ordinary farm is available for conversion into currency. These estimates indicate the relation of the scale of marriage payments to the resources of Yakö households but they cannot be taken to imply that a groom or his father can easily realise the   sum necessary for making a marriage payment.

Non-payment of Marriage Money. During my enquiries concerning   marriage payments I came across a few cases, all very recent, in which,   although no payment or the most trivial token payment had been made, the parents of the bride had permitted her to join her husband and while recognising the marriage had resigned themselves to non-payment of libeman.

In very recent years, mostly since 1935 and mainly owing to the fall of oil prices and the scarcity of currency a number of young men have been unable to obtain sufficient to make even the reduced payment of £1   which has been frequently accepted in full settlement. At the same time   those responsible for the repayment of marriage money on behalf of a wife married several years before who deserted her husband have often been placed   in difficulty. Where as is customary three- or four-fifths of an original marriage payment of £5. 5. 0 is awarded by the Native Court to a deserted husband it has become a very severe tax on the matrilineal kinsman of the wife to amass this amount. Both these considerations are encouraging the recognition of marriage without marriage payment, a practice which I heard described as intrinsically desirable by some younger parents and mother's brothers as giving the young women for whom they were responsible more freedom to leave bad husbands. Already in a few cases there has been   formal

---

[1] The mean figure of a number of sales recorded over this period.

[2] For methods whereby these data were obtained see Forde, Land and Labour in a Cross River Village, S. Nigeria, Geog. Journ., 90,1937, pp.24-51.

recording of such a marriage, or more precisely of the non-payment of marriage money, in the presence of the Ward Head. The father and the mother's brother have told the groom to come with them at an appointed time to the Ward Head (Obot Kekpatū) bringing 2/- to declare that he is marrying without making any marriage payment. The Ward Head calls a writer to whom he gives 1/- for preparing a written statement in English of which one copy is kept by the Ward Head and the other by the wife. The text of one such statement ran: This is to show that the intending husband ... has not paid dowry to me... [father] and she is allowed to go free whenever she wishes to divorce. The eye evidence of those following:
[the names of two messengers of the Ward Head]

Chief .... his (X) mark
Witness to mark and writer ....

This practice has been adopted as a protection against future claims on the wife's kin in the Native Court. The preparation of a written declaration in English shows the influence of the Court procedure in which an English summary of cases is prepared by the Clerk as a record subject to inspection by the Administrative Officer.

Although reduction and, in a few cases omission, of marriage payment have eased the stress during the recent years of shrunken money incomes, disputes over marriage payments have not thereby been eliminated. Indeed they are said by the older men to be more frequent than in the old days when every one knew how much the libeman was and the chiefs (i.e. the village head and leaders of the matriclans constituting the Yabŏt) could judge quickly and compel payment within a reasonable time.

An example from Umor which extended over my two periods of work among the Yakö will serve to indicate the setting and some of the complications involved in such disputes. A girl Eni of age-set XVII was living with a sister of her mother in Idjiman ward as her own parents were dead. She became betrothed in 1933 to a youth Usani of Idjum who made a betrothal gift of 10/- in lieu of farm services to her mother's senior brother Okoi. In 1934 before the Lebokū rites she had a likpŏkŏt wedding as she was already pregnant but no marriage payment was made. Her child was born at the end of the year, while she was still in her maternal aunt's house, but died when only a month old. A few months later at the end of the planting season (about May) in 1935 her junior maternal uncle, Ubi - her mother's senior brother having died in the meantime - went to the groom's father to remind him that the marriage money had not been paid at likpŏkŏt and it was time it should be handed over. The father promised to come on the next kokŏ to settle the amount on his son's behalf and make a first payment. He came, but brought only a calabash of palm wine asking Ubi to be patient as he had no money. About a month later the father fell suddenly ill and died. After the funeral rites Ubi went to the groom, Usani, reminding him he would have to provide the marriage money. He said he had no money yet but would pay later.

During this farming season Ūsani built Eni a house in his late   father's
compound and she went to live there after the harvest. The bride's   maternal
aunt came to tell her brother Ubi of this saying it would soon be time for Eni
to go and plant her husband's first farm. She urged that Ubi should let   her
do this and stay in the house Ūsani had provided although the marriage payment
had not yet been made. As Eni was again pregnant and Ubi hoped Ūsani wouldmake
the payment during the coming year he agreed. Ūsani had a small farm plot in
which he planted only 20 to 25 sticks of yams.

Eni's second child was born before the harvest of 1936. This secondchild,
a boy, was also sickly and died in the following planting season early in 1937
while Eni herself was very ill. She came to Ubi during the farming season in
about July 1937 to say that she wanted to join some friends who were going to
Agoi Ibami, a village about twelve miles east of Umor, to consult a well-known
magician in the hope of finding out why her children died.This magician performed the Itenga divination with strings of native mango seed shells and she
returned from Agoi to tell Ubi that the magician had said that it was becaus e
her mother's brother's breast had not cooled from the anger at the refusal of
her husband to pay the marriage money that her children had died. He had told
her to tell her husband to give her mother's brother a back leg of smoked antelope, and a 4 sectioned kola to take to the priest of her matriclanclanshrine
for the performance of the 'cooling' rite in which the priest and elders of the
clan spray water on the patient at dawn on a kokö day. Ubi called the husband
Ūsani to his house, asked if he had been told by his wife of the instructions
of the Itenga magician. He said he had, was willing to provide the meat   for
the rite and would do so when he next went to Agoi to buy bush meat for trading. But a month later Emi came to her mother's brother again and said   she
could not persuade her husband to fulfil his promise and when she pressed him
he had said he was tired of her and her mother's brother and their   continual
requests. Ubi then sent for him again and he came only at a second calling to
deny that he had refused to provide meat for the ceremony.

Eni was pregnant again at the beginning of 1938, her husband had   still
brought no offering for the 'cooling' rite. Before the harvest of 1938   Eni
bore a girl child who died in a few days and Ubi went to Ūsani in great   anger
saying:- "This is the third child that has died. You remember what the magician said. All these children of our matriclan, are dying because of   your
greediness and laziness." The husband appeared contrite, asked Ubi to forgive
him and promised to make the offering within one or two kokös while Eni declared before her mother's brother that he must make the offering before they had
intercourse again. In a few days, however, Ūsani told his wife he had no money
to buy the leg of antelope and tried to sleep with her. She came to Ubi   to
tell him and he ordered her to go back and fetch her belongings from the house
at once. She did so and Ubi gave her an empty woman's house in his own   compound to live in. In a day or two the husband came to Ubi bringing a calabash
of wine and accompanied by two messengers of the head of Ubi's ward and one of
the Village Head to whom he had appealed. Ūsani had complained of the alleged

desertion of his wife at the instigation of her mother's brother asserting
that he had treated her well but concealing both the dispute over the payment of marriage money and his breach of promise about the 'cooling' rite.
The messengers urged Ubi to allow his wife to return while Usani promised
before them to make the offering for the 'cooling' rite at the shrine   of
her matriclan. Ubi agreed that she should return to her husband.

A little after the harvest Eni told Ubi that Usani had said he would
not make the offering and had abused Ubi to her. Ubi then went with her to
the Village Head and then to the Head of his ward to tell them his version
of the dispute. They agreed that he might take Eni away from Usani and he
did so immediately. Usani came again with several friends and calabashes
of wine asking Ubi to relent. Ubi refused saying that Eni would not return
to Usani until he had provided the offering for performing the ceremony. He
returned the next day and again a few days later to plead for his wife's
return but Ubi refused to budge and on the last occasion said that   Usani
was to go to his yam stack with him and Eni to point out her yams so that
they might be carried to the stack of one of their matrilineal kinsmen who
farmed on that path. Usani refused to do this and Ubi then went to one of
the senior elders of Usani's patriclan to tell him of the decision of the
Village Head and to complain of Usani's conduct. Ubi was not prepared to
take the yams without having them pointed out lest he be accused of theft
or cause a fight at the stack. The old men of Usani's patriclan said it
was not good for Eni to leave her husband and tried to put Ubi off,   pro-
mising to influence Usani to behave properly and saying that they   would
send him to comply with Ubi's wishes and beg for the return of his wife.
Usani came next day but Eni herself said she would not return to him   unless Ubi told her to, while Ubi insisted that Usani must make the offering
first. Both men were completely obstinate on this point and Usani   went
away. This was early in 1939 when the new farms were being cleared   and
planting was beginning so that Ubi wished to make arrangements for planting Eni's yams. He therefore went to the head of Biko Biko ward, not of
his own ward as he wanted an independent arbitrator, to ask one of the
head's messengers to act as a witness as he wished to take away Eni's yams
from Usani's yam stack. The ward head knew of the dispute and agreed to
send his man the next day and said he would call the husband to go too. He
called Usani and told him to come the next morning and take the party to the
stack and see for himself that only Eni's yams were taken. Usani said he
did not wish to separate from his wife and tried again to reopen the whole
question alleging that he had given the deceased senior mother's brother
one pound as a marriage payment. Ubi and his friends successfully insisted that only ten shillings had been given and that this was in lieu of farm
services and not marriage money. It was arranged that a messenger of the
Biko Biko ward head should go the next day to witness the removal of the
yams. Usani was at the stack when they arrived the next morning and made
no trouble except to claim as his one of Eni's water pots left there, and
the yams were carried to another part of the same yam stack where a matri-

lineal kinsman of Ūbi and Eni, who was also a patrilineal kinsman of the husband, stored his yams.

A few days later Ūsani went to the village head claiming repayment of one pound for betrothal gifts given to Eni and her mother's brother before their marriage. The village head sent a messenger to summon Eni, that he might hear the dispute. Ūbi refused to let her go saying that if there was to be any further dispute Ūsani could summon her in the Native Court. Ūsani next tried to have Eni summoned before the Ukpakapi ward head _ for the same purpose, but Ūbi made the same answer to the messenger. Ūsani made no further attempt to recover his wife or claim any repayment for betrothal gifts.

During the later phase of this dispute after the harvest of 1938 and before Ūbi went to the elder of Ūsani's patriclan another man Otū of Biko Biko ward (age-set XVII) and sought Eni as a wife. He first approached Ūbi who told him that Eni would not return to her former husband who had not paid libeman and that he could offer marriage to Eni. Otū was one of several men who had suggested marriage with Eni after she had arrived in Ūbi's compound. Ūbi refused the others because he thought them of poor promise as husbands. Otū already had one wife. The next day he came to Ūbi accompanied by his foster-father who said he had brought a _ calabash of palm wine to show that Otū was earnest in his offer for Eni. Ūbi agreed that Eni should go to Otū if she were willing but that a marriage payment must be made and he would accept one pound. The foster-father agreed and Ūbi then asked Otū what Eni had said when he (Otū) had approached her. Otū replied that Eni had expressed her readiness to accept him and' Ūbi then called her. She said she would accept any husband Ūbi chose for her. Ūbi refused this answer and asked if she wished to go to Otū. She then said she was willing and Otū offered to get friends to carry her yams from the stack on the Idjum side of the village to his own house. Ūbi then asked for payment of the marriage money. Otū and his foster-father replied that they would pay later on, but could not do so at once. Ūbi did not press for immediate payment lest Otū should think he was not really willing for Eni to go to him, for he was anxious that she should be settled with a good husband, but he told Otū that he must, in order that Eni might bear healthy children, produce the back leg of smoked antelope, kola _ and wine for the ceremony at the shrine as presented by the magician. Otū agreed to do so on the next kokö and the yams were carried by Otū and his friends to Otū's house.

On the next kokö Otū duly brought the offering to Ūbi's compound. Eni and Otū with Ūbi and two oe three of the latter's age mates then went to the priest's compound where he was waiting for them. The priest was of the same patrilineage as Eni's former husband Ūsani, but the former had not informed Ūsani that the rite was to be held.

The priest was accompanied by two elders of the matriclan.He brought out a calabash bowl about a foot diameter, poured water into it and into the water a few drops of oil and some powdered chalk. He first sprinkled water from the bowl on to the ground all round and then took up a piece of raphia stem which he split lengthwise into pieces. Taking one of these he touched first his lips and then the rim of the bowl and said "This was bad speech we have been using" and threw it to one side. He then repeated the action with another raphia stick saying "This is good speech we are using today" and dropped the stick into the water. The same action was then repeated by the elders and all Ūbi's party who sat round the bowl throughout. The priest next took up the calabash and sucked some of the water into his mouth and the other men present did the same. Eni extended her hands,palms upwards, and all simultaneously sprayed water on them. The men then went over to the shade in the priests compound where the meat and kola were shared and wine drunk.

That night Otū came and slept with Eni in Ūbi's compound and she became pregnant two or three moons later. Otū had her help in planting his farm and she took some of her yams to plant in his farm. The rest were planted in Ubi's farm. Otū handed to Ūbi the agreed marriage payment during the cultivating season and was building Eni a house in his own compound before the harvest.

CHAPTER X

THE ESTABLISHMENT OF A HOUSEHOLD

It has already been indicated that a wife after her first   marriage
does not usually come to reside or work with her husband for a considerable period, and in general not until after her first child has been born.
Wives first join their husbands as a rule at a particular time   of year
which is determined by the seasonal sequence of agricultural   operations
and by the appropriate time for housebuilding which is also largely   dependent on farming activities.

Occasionally when a nubile girl is not well treated in her own household, she may join her husband soon after or even before the   clitorodectomy rite. Thus a girl Otu of age set XVI in Umor was living   in her
father's household in the care of a step-mother with whom she got on very
badly. When she became pregnant the youth to whom she was betrothed, who
was himself living in the household of his mother's brother, secured   a
house for her there. As her mother was dead one of her matrilineal kinswomen acted in her stead during the marriage rites and the father   came
with his friends to the husband's compound when likpokot was performed.

The bridegroom has to provide the woman's house ready for his wife to
live in. He may be offered the house of a divorced or recently deceased
wife of a patrilineal kinsman, but often a new house has to be built and
this can only be done during the season of housebuilding and repairing which
occupies the months between the Leboku rites, in late June or July,   and
the main yam harvest which begins early in November. At this time of year
men have a respite from daily work on their farms and greater opportunity
to collect the supplies of raphia poles and other wood, puddled mud and
palm fronds required for housebuilding. The task of collecting and fabri-
cating the materials is nearly always carried out by one or more groups of
kinsmen and age mates of the house-builder although the work of moulding
the mud platforms and benches inside the house is commonly done by special-
ists who today are paid a fee of two or three shillings for their work.

At his first marriage a youth will generally have the direct aid of
his father in organising and obtaining workers for the task of housebuilding. In Umor, owing to the fact that most of the clumps of raphia palms,
which are planted trees, are owned collectively by groups of matrilineal
kinsmen ranging from part of a lineage to a whole clan, permission for cutting supplies of the long raphia midribs for the wall frames and the roof
structure will have to be sought by taking a token gift of wine to the
elders controlling the raphia clumps belonging to the matrilineal kin of
the husband or of his father. A party of the husband's patriclan (kepun)
fellows or age mates will usually help him to cut and carry in the raphia
poles and also the large bundles of oil palm fronds, collected in the palm

collecting territory of the husband or his father, which are needed to make the hundred or more mats required for roofing a house. They too will join in digging out clay from a convenient pit for daubing the walls and providing material for the platforms and benches. The father and a few of his patriclan friends will direct the construction of a house for a youthful husband and his mother with her friends and sometimes the bride's mother with her friends will carry out the woman's task of daubing the walls. As a rule all this work progresses but slowly in the intervals between other occupations, and it is often two months or more before a house is completed. The house should, however, be ready before the opening of the farming year in which the wife is to join her husband in farm work.

The provision of utensils for the new household is as a rule left to the wife and her parents who should supply a set of pots, mortars, head bowls and baskets which she will bring with her on coming to reside in her husband's compound. This equipment should include at least one large iron stew pot and also a set of enamel bowls which, while only occasionally used, are regarded as an essential decoration for the back wall of the house - the equivalent of best china displayed on the dresser in a farm kitchen. On the other hand it is the duty of the husband to provide his wife's hoes and other equipment for farm work, such as storage baskets.

The provision of farming land for the new household now becomes necessary. The father of the groom will often be able to provide a plot from a portion of his own farming tract for that year. If not he will go at the opening of the new farming season to the patriclan elder in charge of the farm path on which he himself farms to tell him that he is seeking a plot for his son to make his first farm. At the meeting of the farm path elder and the men farming on his path which is called every year, for the discussion of new claims and adjustments in holdings, a portion will be allotted to the young husband and in the early part of the dry season, late in January, he will join bush clearing parties which will help to clear his first farm.

The provision of planting yams for the new farming unit is a joint responsibility of the parents of the husband and the wife. The parents of both should give sticks of yams from their own harvest stores when planting begins. Among the Yakö, although the working of a farm is a joint enterprise of a husband and his wife or wives, each retains property rights in his or her own yams. The yams of a husband and of each wife are planted in separate sections of the farm and are marked and kept separate when harvested. As the early varieties of yams (lidjōfi) which provide food from June to October are generally owned only by women a bride will be expected to receive from her mother and bring to the new farm an adequate supply of these in addition to main crop yams. Thus a husband will receive about half a dozen sticks of main harvest yams from his father and two or three from his mother while a wife will expect two or three sticks of main harvest yams from her father and one or two from her mother together with two or more sticks of early yams. A stick of yams, so called because yams are tied to vertical poles to a height of about ten feet for storage in the harvest stacks, consists of about 30 medium sized yams. The lesser farm crops such as corn, beans, okra and coco-yams are also women's crops. The wife owns and controls the harvests and the supplies for new plant- ings of these foods although she is at the same time under obligation to provide her husband and children with adequate supplies of them during the the year. Of all these a woman will ask for a supply for planting from her mother and/or of her mother's sisters.

While the various farming tasks are carried out over a farm as a whole the yams of a man and those of his wife or wives are, as has been said, planted and harvested separately. They are tied on distinct groups of uprights in the husband's harvest stack. Each has a distinctive mark which is incised on the base of the yams as they are dug at harvest time and the separate harvests of each are used in turn to provide household food accord- ing to well established rules. Thus during the harvesting of the main crop which usually extends over two moons in November and December the digging and tying of yams is done by the husband while the washing and carrying of yams to the stack is the task of the wife and friends who may help her. The husband digs his own yams first. He then goes on to dig those of his wife or if he has more than one wife for each in turn on successive days until the work is done. During the harvest period yams for the daily food are taken from the husband's or the wife's harvest according to which is being dug at the time. When the yams are about to be tied to the uprights in the harvest barn a wife is entitled to take the equivalent of one stick of medium sized yams equally from her own and her husband's crops as they lie spread out to dry off in the sun. These are tied separately from the rest of the harvest and are used for food in the period immediately fol- lowing. When they are exhausted a wife is expected to use two sticks of her own yams before asking for more from her husband. The husband should then supply two sticks and these five sticks or about 150 medium sized yams in all, are considered to be sufficient for ordinary food supplies for a wife and children and her husband for the three months from December un- til the new planting season has began in early March. The bodies of the yams whose bases are used for the new planting are then available for food as the work progresses. After planting the household will depend on a re- serve of yams not used for planting which is now carried into the village to be stored in the house and used for food from late April until late July when, after the Lebokū rites, the early yams of that year may be dug. To this reserve a husband should contribute four or five sticks and a wife two or three. The early yams from which the household food is obtained for three or four months from mid-July until the main harvest beginning in November are usually, as has been seen, provided only by the wife but they are the sole source for the household if, as is generally the case, practically all the yams of the last harvest have already been eaten.

68

A husband will during the period of betrothal and in the early months of marriage usually become an intimate of his wife's parents' household.He may talk freely to and before his mother-in-law who will give him food and ask him for gifts. There is neither avoidance nor any exceptional intimacy. A man may, if there is need and relations are good, continue to give his father-in-law occasional help in farm clearing, housebuilding and other work after he has taken his wife to live with him in the area of his own kepun.

The pattern of personal relations between affinal relatives does not appear to be specific among the Yakö. Towards their parents-in-law both man and wife behave in general as they would to senior kinsfolk and the considerable variation in the degree of intimacy and sympathy between affines appears to depend on the temperamental qualities of the persons involved. Sexual relations with an affinal relative are regarded as highly improper, but most informants said that there was no specific penalty for it because it would not occur, and I did not in fact encounter any instance in marital histories, court records, or discussions of sexual irregularities.

A wife has normally more frequent contact with her parents-in-law than does a husband. The wife-father-in-law relation often becomes one of considerable affection. A man may frequently be seen gossiping in his daughter-in-law's house and I have noticed a young wife during a discussion in the compound stand leaning an arm over her father-in-law's shoulder - a posture that a daughter might adopt in public but never a wife. A young wife may also be asked by her mother-in-law to help in a farm or compound task and will generally be ready to do so, but such help is an expression of regard not an obligatory service.

CHAPTER XI

DISSOLUTION OF MARRIAGE

Death. At the death of a married man or woman the yams he or she owns whether still tied in the harvest stack or growing in the farm pass to the heirs who are successors to moveable property, that is to one or more matrilineal 'sons or daughters' of the deceased and not to the surviving spouse.

When a wife dies both her rights and her duties in her husband's farm fall for the rest of the farming year to her close matrilineal kinswomen who should take her place in completing the woman's labour on the farm. If she dies before the harvest her husband goes to her mother's brother and asks to be given the services of one or more of her 'sisters' to work in the farm and carry in the harvest. But when the yams are harvested those of the deceased wife are not tied in the husband's stack. They are carried away by her 'sisters' for distribution among themselves and their matrilineal relatives. If she dies after harvest but before the opening of the next farming year her yams in the husband's stack are claimed at planting time by her matrilineal kin usually by a sister or grown daughter, but the husband may claim and retain a share necessary for feeding any of her young children that are remaining in his household.

At the end of the farming season the responsibilities to her husband of the dead woman's matrikin are ended. There can be no legal claim for return of the marriage payment from the wife's mother's brother and no return is usually made, I was, however, told that if a wife were to die within a very short time of marriage the widower could through his patrikins-men bring pressure on the mother's brother to make him a substantial gift of consolation which would in fact be part of the payment made. The Yakö have no form of sororate. A man is free to marry a woman of the matrilineage of his deceased wife, and may seek to make a smaller marriage payment in such a case, but there is no legal obligation on the former wife's kin to offer another spouse or to accept less marriage money.

When a man dies his household usually continues to function as an economic unit until the end of the farming year, but his widow, although she will continue to work on his farm until the harvest, can claim only a share of his yams sufficient to contribute to feeding any of his young children that will remain in her care. On their behalf too she can later ask for gifts of yams for food from her late husband's brothers and sisters' sons to whom his yam harvest passes. Only if a woman is widowed while suckling a child has she a right to remain in her late husband's compound and to be given farming facilities by one of his patrikin. She may or may not prefer to rejoin her parents or other relatives, but in any case she cannot remarry until she is ready to wean the child and is therefore dependent on either the late husband's or her own relatives for farming facilities and food supplies.

A widow similarly has no personal claim to the livestock and personal possessions of her late husband although she may, at the distribution of his goods during the funeral rites, be given a cloth and a few other small objects by the matrilineal relative of her husband who is the chief heir.

On the other hand a claim is made on the widow by the age set mates (kobpma) of her late husband. The best friend of the dead man requests a money payment from the widow which should be given before the funeral rites are completed. The payment claimed is said to vary according to the amount of the marriage money transferred at her marriage. It should be a third to a half of that amount and where there have been disputes over these payments judgments for as much as a half of the marriage payment have been given by the Village Head and also by the Native Court. But the payments actually made during recent years in cases known to me have rarely been more than a quarter of the original marriage payment while from elderly widows of old men only token payments appear to be expected.

The widow's matrilineage, and in particular that kinsman, usually the mother's brother, who received the major portion of the marriage payment, are legally responsible for ensuring the payment, if necessary by providing the amount agreed. But it is held that if the widow's father had retained the entire marriage payment at the time of marriage, her mother's brother can justifiably refuse to provide the widow with the means of making the payment to her dead husband's age mates on the ground that by retaining the marriage payment the father had assumed responsibility for all his daughter's obligations as a wife.

It might be thought that this payment is a transfer of property which completes the cycle initiated by the original payment of marriage money, but this view is neither present in the minds of the Yakö nor consistent with their attitudes to marriage payment and to succession in property rights. The payment to the age mates is described by the Yakö as a consolation of the dead man's age set for their loss. The age mates have no right to inherit any of the dead man's property or to succeed to his marital rights. On the other hand his sisters' sons who are his heirs claim no payment from the widow or her mother's brother nor do his sons for the provision of whose marriage payments the dead man has been or would later have been responsible. It is consistent with the Yakö principles of the obligations of matrilineal kinship that the mother's brother of the widow should be responsible for ensuring the payment, but the payment itself, although it is linked in amount with the marriage payment, cannot be regarded as a liquidation of the obligations which the latter involved.

A man's patrikin have on the other hand no claim on the person or services of his widow after the end of the farming season in which he   died. The levirate is as foreign to the Yakö as is the sororate.

At the death of her husband the widow no longer keeps her hair clipped short in the Yakö fashion adopted by women young and old, but allows it to grow so that it can be twisted up in a large number of spikes   all over the head (ngpuna) in exactly the same fashion as that adopted by a bride who is in seclusion after the kekpopam rite at her first marriage. She should continue to adopt this hair style for a year after her husband's death.

A young widow usually remarries within a year or two. She leaves her late husband's compound after the harvest following his death and   joins the household of either her parents or of a matrikinsman such as a brother or mother's brother. Older widows who have adult sons living in the patriclan area and usually in the same compound as the late husband, often remain in their houses and join the farming units of the sons, who are of course their closest matrilineal kinsmen. But I found several   instances in which woman who were widowed late in life, several years after   menopause, had remarried. Such women are, according to native statements, including those of men who had married widows of mature years, sought   as companions and farm and household workers by older men who have lost wives and no longer desire either a lover or bearer of children.

Divorce occurs frequently among the Yakö today and, as will be seen, a very large proportion of adult women have permanently separated   from their first husbands in recent times. Divorce results both from dismissal of the wife by her husband and from desertion of the husband, often in order to join another lover, on the part of the wife. The Yakö pattern of domestic relations is one of marked male dominance and, while this by no means always exists in practice, disobedience, violent temper and quarrelsomeness of a wife are in general opinion sufficient grounds for dismissing her and claiming return of part at least of the marriage money.   In practice it has, at least in recent years, been difficult if not impossible for a husband to secure the return of marriage money after dismissing a wife until she has gone to live as a wife with another man, but   the claim is held to be valid and can be successfully made even after a lapse of several years when the woman does join another man. A wife's delinquency, such as adultery, recurrent theft of yams from farms or   harvest stores of the husband or others, is also regarded as adequate grounds for her dismissal, but much will depend on the actual circumstances and   temperament of the married pair as to whether the husband will in fact   divorce his wife in such circumstances. There appears to be little   pressure of opinion on the part of kinsmen or friends which would compel   a man to dismiss a wife for sexual offenses. Adultery entitles a man in Yakö custom to chastise his wife and to claim a fine, formerly a goat or even

a cow from the adulterer, but of itself adultery appears rarely to result
in divorce.

When a man determines on dismissing a wife he informs both her   and
her parents or close matrilineal kin that she must go. If she does   not
do so, taking with her her household belongings and her yams in the husband's stack, he can refuse to admit her to his farm in the coming year.
Her position is then untenable. She is compelled to seek other means of
providing for herself and her relatives will in fact take her away.

But divorces result in the great majority of cases from the voluntary
departure of the wife from her husband's compound. At the same time the
departure of a wife after a quarrel with her husband by no means   always
ends in permanent divorce. To leave her house with her young children and
go to stay with one or other of her close relatives breaking off all   relations with her husband including work on his farm is a weapon frequently employed by a wife who considers herself unfairly treated and seeks to
coerce her husband. The dislocation which this is likely to cause in his
household and farming arrangements are often sufficient to induce the husband to seek her return through the intervention of her kinsfolk. For a
wife to remove her belongings from her house and her yams from her   husband's store is, however, a declaration of her intention to end the marriage. This is sometimes done when the woman has already secretly arranged to become the wife of another man, but in any case she will go   first
to a relative, usually a matrikinsman, who will give her a woman's house
to live in; and she will as a rule take up residence with a new mate only
at the beginning of a farming year. If a woman deserts her husband and,
after an interval, goes to live with another man, her new mate   becomes
liable to make a payment to the matrilineal kinsman who has the   obligation to refund wholly or in part the marriage payment of the first husband.
In fact divorce may be said to be established among the Yakö only when an
agreed portion of the marriage payment in connection with the earlier marriage has been returned. This in practice is, at the present time at least,
rarely done until the wife has joined a new mate and after persistent requests have been made by the husband which often end in either a claim before the ward or village head or an action in the Native Court. A wife may
desert her husband and stay with relatives for several years during which
the original marital relation is suspended but not annulled.

A few examples of the circumstances attending particular divorces will
make the situation more clear. At the opening of the farming year in January 1935 Ūsani, a middle aged man (age-set X) of Ūkpakapi ward in   Umor
brought to his compound as an additional wife a woman of Idjūm ward   who
had left her first husband two years before and was living in the compound
of one of her matrilineal kinsmen on whose farm she had worked. The woman
brought with her when she joined Ūsani, her two girl children of six and
four years old whom she had brought away when she left her former husband.

Her other child boy of seven she had left with her husband. The husband
went to the village head together with her matrilineal kinsman about two
months later to demand that Ūsani should make a payment of £4.10. 0, the
amount of the original marriage payment. Ūsani insisted that as the woman
had borne three children to her first husband and had also been away from
him for two years without his securing her return there was no longer any
just claim for return of any of the original payment. The husband saidhe
had always been willing to have the woman back and offered to do so now.
She refused, describing many alleged incidents in which he had neglected
her interests in farm work and claiming that he had in fact accepted her
departure since he had not come to ask her to return to him. Moreover he
had since her departure taken another wife who was a woman of her own patrilineage which was both an insult to her and a breach of custom, if the
former marriage was not void, since a man may not marry a woman of the same
lineage as one who is already his wife. The village head appears to have
agreed that the former husband had no longer any claim on the woman but
held that Ūsani should make a marriage payment to the woman's matrilineal
kinsman. This did not however settle the dispute for Ūsani made no such
payment while the former husband was still aggrieved. The latter summoned Ūsani before the Native Court where, according to a practice which the
older men say is not traditional but has grown up in recent years,   the
former husband claimed for a refund of his marriage payment direct from
Ūsani whom his wife had joined. The court awarded £3.10.0 to the first
husband but did not fix a time within which it had to be paid and only a
few shillings which were then handed over as a first instalment had in
fact been paid four years later in 1939.

A man of Idjum ward of age-set XV had a sick wife. Her ailment was
described as a 'swollen heart' and she was for a time unable to go regularly to work in the farm. The husband went to her father and asked him
to take her back and have the marriage money refunded as she was no longer fit to be his wife. The father refused but shortly after the woman
left on her own initiative. After staying with her parents for three
months she joined a man of Biko Biko ward. Her husband discovered this
through seeing his second child by this wife playing in Biko Biko and asking child where he and his mother were staying. He then summoned before
the Native Court the man who had taken his wife claiming a refund of his
marriage payment of £5. 5. 0. In Court the wife asserted that only £2 had
been paid and that in any case her former husband had driven her from him
without justification. The man to whom she had gone said that his own
former wife had died during farm clearing time and that he had failed to
get satisfactory help from her matrilineal kinswomen. He had met the woman in the compound of a friend, who at the request of her parents had giv-
en her the use of an empty woman's house he then had, and asked her to help
him on his farm offering her a place to plant her yams. She agreed only
on condition that he took her as a wife. After first denying it he admitted that he knew that her former husband was alive and living in Umor.

He was ordered to pay over £1.10. 0 to the former husband in settlement of his claim for a refund of marriage payment.

A young woman from Ūkpakapi ward contracted leprosy and her husband wishing to divorce her on that account told her to leave and go back to her mother's house and demanded the return of the marriage payment. The ward head of Ūkpakapi, who was appealed to by the husband, approved the claim and ordered return of the marriage payment to the husband. The wife refused to leave her husband's compound crying and struggling when he and others approached her. Finally after a quarrel she ran out of the compound and along a farming path where several hours later she was found where she had hanged herself from a tree.

Arikpo of Idjūm ward, of age set XII, first married Omini making a marriage payment of £6. 5. 0 on the day of her likpŏkot rite. Her father kept £3 and gave £3 to her adult full brother (his son) as matrilineal kinsman as well as the customary gift of 5/- to her age mates. Two years later Arikpo made a marriage payment of £5. 5. 0 for a second wife Odjeika at her kekpopam rite. His first wife Omini had been nursing a child during his betrothal to Odjeika and weaned it shortly after Odjeika went into seclusion as an ŏkpŏlŏkpŏla. Arikpo who spent many of his nights with Odjeika in her house suspected that Omini was being unfaithful to him and quarrelled with her frequently over this. Friends who saw her going about at night continued to tell him of it and finally, when he went back to his compound in the middle of the night on one occasion to get a gift for a club which was holding an all night dance in Odjeika's compound, he found that Omini was not in her house. She refused next morning to tell him where she had been, there was another angry quarrel and Arikpo told her to leave. This she did going to stay with her brother and taking the child with her. After a few days he went to the brother and asked without success for return of his marriage payment. Still later he went again this time insisting that he should receive back his payment or that Omini should return to work on his farm. As Omini refused to return to him and the brother would give no undertaking Arikpo went to the village head offering a fee of 2/- asking for his claim to be heard. The village head called together some of the Yabot, or village council, and summoned Omini and her brother before him. On hearing the case the village head ordered that Omini must return to Arikpo or the brother must return the marriage payment within three moons. After some delay and threats of an action in the Native Court the brother finally paid back £5 to Arikpo. The boy child of this marriage remained with its mother who is likely to marry again but her brother intends to bring him up as his foster-son and to adopt him into his patriclan.

Consideration of these and other histories of marital disputes, including cases heard in the Native Court, permit the following general statements about divorce among the Yakŏ at the present time. The older practice whereby the matrilineal kinsmen, or more recently and in some cases, the father of the wife, took responsibility for the return of the marriage payment if the wife failed in her marital duties,is giving place to one in which return of marriage payment to a husband whose wife has left him can be secured only from a man who takes the woman to live with him as a wife. There is today rarely any marriage payment as such when a divorced woman joins a new spouse. What is claimed is a sum with which to compensate the former husband for the marriage payment originally made by him. Traditionally the responsibility for providing this lies with the mother's brother of the woman who in turn would demand a marriage payment of any man who wishes subsequently to take the woman as a wife. In practice the question of repayment of marriage money is often raised only after the woman has joined another man and the husband is reimbursed directly by him.

If a marriage is dissolved after several children have been born a husband is considered by ward and village heads and by the Native Court bench as entitled to return of only a portion of the original marriage payment, usually little more than half.

When a woman leaves her husband she is rarely prevented in practice from taking very young children with her, but she is rarely allowed to take older boy children and the husband often demands that young male children shall return to him when they reach puberty. If a woman deserting her husband brings young children with her when she comes to live with another man, the man can claim a reduction of the amount of payment whether it be to her former husband or to her matrilineal kinsmen on the ground that he is supporting these children.

The Frequency of Divorce. That divorce has in recent times had a high incidence among the Yakö can be seen from the sample of marital histories summarised in Table 5. Of the total sample of 313 women of ages ranging from 17 to over 70 years, 121 have already been divorced at least once.

If we confine our attention to the 98 women in the sample who have reached late middle age and been married for over twenty years, i.e. those of age-set XI, c.40 years of age in 1939, or older, it will be seen that 28% were divorced either prior to or after their marriages to men of the Ndai patriclan from whom the data were obtained. This is not however a satisfactory index of the present divorce rate since although divorce becomes increasingly infrequent with age some of the wives may still be divorced in the future and it does not include divorces of younger wives. In fact of the 152 younger married women in the sample of age sets XII to XVI i.e. between approximately 36 and 22 years of age in 1939, 38 or 25% had already been divorced at least once in their marital history. It therefore appears from this sample that the divorce rate has been increasing in Umor and that at the present time at least 30% of women are divorced at least once in their marital history.

TABLE 5 Marital History of Women Married to Men of Ndai Patriclan.
by Age Sets I – XVIII

Status at Marriage to Ndai Man	Still married to Ndai Husband			Widowed			Divorced			Deceased			Total
*	Y	D	W	Y	D	W	Y	D	W	Y	D	W	
I												1	1
II												1	1
III										1			1
IV	2			1					1	4	2		10
V	1	2			1	1	3		1	4		1	14
VI	5	2	4				3	1		2			17
VII	1	1	1				1			3			7
VIII	2	2	2	1			3			2		1	13
IX					1		2	2	1	1			7
X	6	7	3	1	1		4	1		4			27
XI	7	4	2				8	1	1	2		1	26
XII	9	9	1	1			4	1		4			29
XIII	13	7	4		1		8			1			34
XIV	7	4	1				2						14
XV	15	6		1			8	4		4			38
XVI	26	5		1			4	1					37
XVII	25						1						26
XVIII	11												11
	130	49	18	6	4	1	51	11	4	32	2	5	313
		197			11			66			39		

* Y = unmarried; D = Divorcee; W = Widow

A

There is among the Yakö no limitation apart from inclination and the resources commanded on the number of wives that a man may have at any one time, and, as will be seen, demographic conditions have in recent times been favourable to a high incidence of polygyny. Plural marriage is an undoubted advantage to an energetic man who has access to tracts of land adequate for cultivating a large farm every year or is active in the collection of oil palm products for preparation and sale. Many men in Umor have farms considerably larger than could be maintained with the aid of only one wife, for although the labour of visiting Ezza Ibo youths can be obtained for the work of hoeing up yam hills, female labour is essential for weeding the farm, cultivating secondary crops and carrying the yam harvest, I was in fact frequently told by men in explanation of certain of their later marriages that increase in their yam harvests or the death of one wife made it necessary for them to seek another wife without delay. Plural marriage is also valued as a means of rearing a larger number of children and so of increasing the strength of a man's patrilineage and of his own prestige within it.

On the other hand there is little emphasis on the number of wives as a direct expression of a man's importance and prestige. The priestleaders of the clans both patrilineal and matrilineal for example are not distinguished by a markedly higher degree of polygyny than the adult male population in general. Thus investigation of the households of the patrilineal and matrilineal priest-chiefs of Umor in 1935 showed that the 23 patriclan priest heads had 46 living wives residing with them or an average of two per man, while only one had four wives and eight had only one wife each. Similarly the eleven ase (matriclan) priests including the village head and the village speaker (okpebri) had 21 living wives in all or an average of just under two per head. Only two of them had three wives and none had more, while three of them had only one wife.[1] These numbers, as will be

---

[1] Nor do traders, although some have considerable resourses and enjoy a higher standard of material comfort, constitute a distinct class with regard to the number of wives. Trading as a specialist occupation to the exclusion of farming is exceptional among the Yakö. In Umor with over 1800 adult males there are probably not more than two dozen full time traders and most of these are not permanently divorced from farming activities but resume it from time to time when trading returns are poor. The two largest scale full-time traders in Umor each had two wives in 1939. One a man of age set XI,c.40 years old in 1939,who had not farmed for fifteen years or more had two wives,one a Yakö woman with two children who did not farm but herself engaged in petty trading in the Umor market, and the other a foreign woman of the riverside village of Adun recently married, who had lost her child after birth and was still living with her parents in Adun. All food supplies for this trader's household were purchased. Yams were bought in large quantities at harvest and planting times and in smaller amounts during the early yam season. The other large scale trader also had two wives. These wives did however farm. They worked in the farms of matri kinsmen and in these they planted their yams and other crops. Further yam supplies, corresponding to the husband's supply in a normal household were purchased.

seen, are not significantly greater than the incidence of polygyny in the village in general as judged by a sample obtained from the adult men of one section of a large patriclan in Umor in 1939.[1] From Table 6 in which

TABLE 6   Number of Wives living with Husbands of Ndai Patriclan, 1939

Age Set and approx. age of Husband		Number of Wives 1	2	3	4	Totals Men	Wives	Mean number of Wives per Husband		Men without Wives in 1939
I	80 (Years)									1
II	76									1
III	72	1		1		2	4	2.0		
IV	68		1			1	2	2.0		
V	64	3	1	1		5	8	1.6	1.6	
VI	60	4	1	1		6	9	1.5		
VII	56	1	1			2	3	2.0		1
VIII	52	4	1	1		6	9	1.5		2 +
IX	48	1				1	1	1.0		
X	44	6	3		1	10	16	1.6		
XI	40	2	5	2		9	18	2.0		2
XII	36	7	4	2	1	14	25	1.8	2.0	2 +
XIII	32	1	2	1		4	8	2.0		
XIV	29	5	4	2	1	12	23	1.9		
XV	26	5	7	3	3	18	40	2.2		1 +
XVI	23	7	5	1		13	20	1.5		
XVII	20	7	3	1		11	16	1.5	1.4	
XVIII*	18	6	1			7	8	1.1		
		60	39	16	6	121	210	1.7		10

* only married men only of this age set are included.
+ including 1 bachelor.

[1] An earlier sample from this same kin group obtained in 1935 and published in Notes on Some Population Data from a Southern Nigerian Village, Soc.Rev.,30,1938 gave similar results.

the results are analysed it will be seen that among 121 married heads of
households of all ages in the Ndai patriclan the mean number of actual wives
per household is 1.7. The polygyny rate tends to be highest among the
men of early middle age, i.e. between c.25 and 42 years old, where the
mean number of wives per man in a group of 58 men of the age sets XV to
XI inclusive is 2.0. Among the 33 older men over c.42 years in 1939 the
figure is markedly lower, viz. 1.6.[1] The rate for the 32 young married
men under c.25 years of age is 1.4.

If it be assumed that the social context of polygyny has been broadly stable over the past fifty years these rates indicate that among the
Yako a man takes further wives according to his needs and opportunities
throughout his earlier life but that as old age approaches he does not
marry again and that where the wives of marriages in earlier years prede-
cease him they are not usually replaced. The substantial correctness of
this view was confirmed in the field by the infrequency with which old men
with more than one or two living wives were encountered. Indeed elderly
widowers who, although they maintained their own farms, had not remarried
late in life but were dependent on the aid of daughters or sons' wives for
farm work, were not uncommon. There is thus no tendency among the Yako
for old men as a class to secure a disproportionate number of women as
wives at the expense of younger men.

Young men who either by themselves or through their fathers or other
kinsmen command the resources for second marriage payments may contract a
second marriage very shortly after their first. There is particular in-
ducement for this if the first wife has borne a child, for the child will
normally be suckled for two years during which intercourse between the
parents is forbidden. In such a situation the second wife is, as has been
seen, often a previously unmarried girl. A man of middle age can also if
he wishes take as a later wife a girl who is marrying for the first time.
But most men who contract further marriages in middle age marry widows or
divorcees and I have often heard them express a preference for such marriages on various grounds such as avoidance of large marriage payment and
of the elaborate ceremony of a first marriage, and also greater knowledge
of such a woman's qualities as a housekeeper and farm worker and of her
greater experience in these tasks.

Prolonged bachelorhood is very rare among the Yako and is associated
with physical defect or abnormality of temperament. The three fully adult
bachelors found among the 131 men of the kin group referred to above were
all of this class. I encountered occasional instances of men who had remained bachelors from choice. A man known to me in Umor of age set XI,

---

[1] This leaves out of account four formerly married men who were widowers
in 1939.

who was not disabled or incompetent nor said to be impotent, was still unmarried in 1939 when he was about 32 years old. It was said that he had rarely if ever joined lovers parties as a youth and had never been betrothed. He appeared, and was considered by his kinsmen and friends, to be in no way abnormal apart from his sexual indifference to women, and I discovered no indications of homo-sexuality. This man had his own house and farm plots and the woman's work on his farm was done by a wife of his patrilineal half-brother who planted some of her yams in his farm.Widowers who are still active rarely remain wifeless for more than a single farming year as a rule and it is exceptional to find any but the oldest adult men without wives for a considerable time. There were two very old men in this situation in the patriclan investigated and these were virtually dependents in the households of sons.

The number of wives in households is of course no indication of the number of marriages contracted and in view of the frequency of divorce which has already been indicated it will be realised that some men take new wives at frequent intervals during their lives. Thus in the kin group sample referred to above it will be seen from Table 7 that the mean number of marriages per man for a total group of 128 men is 2.5. The 37 men in the oldest sets i.e. those over 40 showed a mean of 2.9 marriages per head, the 60 middle aged men (c.25-40 years) a mean of 2.6 and the 31 young men under 25 a mean of 1.5. These ratios confirm the existence of the tendency discussed above whereby men contract few further marriages in their later years. The men over 40 in this sample show a mean increase of only 0.3 per head over the men of 25 to 40 years.

TABLE 7 Number of Marriages contracted by Ndai Men by Age Sets

Age Set	Approx. Age 1939	Number of Marriages									Totals		Mean number of marriages per Man		None
		1	2	3	4	5	6	7	8	9	Men	Wives			
I	80 years		1								1	2	2.0		
II	76			1							1	3	3.0		
III	72			1		1					2	8	4.0		
IV	68				1						1	4	4.0		
V	64	1	1	1		1			1		5	19	3.8	2.9	
VI	60	1	3	1	1						6	14	2.3		
VII	56	1		1	1						3	8	2.6		
VIII	52	1	4	1						1	7	21	3.0		1
IX	48		1								1	2	2.0		
X	44	1	4	3	1		1				10	28	2.8		
XI	40	3	3	3	1	1					11	27	2.6		
XII	36	1	7	5	1	1					15	39	2.6		1
XIII	32		1	2	1						4	12	3.0	2.6	
XIV	29	3	5	2	1	1					12	28	2.3		
XV	26	4		8	6						18	52	2.9		1
XVI	23	5	6	2							13	23	1.8		
XVII	20	7	3	1							11	16	1.6	1.5	
XVIII	18	6	1								7	8	1.1		
		34	40	32	14	5	1		1	1	128	314	2.5		3

The polygyny rates discussed above obviously imply that if, as there is no reason to doubt, the patriclan here taken as a sample is character-istic of the village of Umor as a whole, then there has over the period available for study existed a very exceptional sex ratio of marriageable males and females. This abnormal ratio cannot, as has been shown else-where,[1] be ascribed to biological factors including selective mortality. It is, on the contrary, a result of one of the most significant of the external relations of the Yakö in the recent past, namely the acquisi-tion by purchase from foreign traders of young children mostly girls for adoption into the clans of the purchasers. This practice has been cur-tailed in recent years by Government action under the Slave Dealing Or-dinances but the data presented here on polygyny among the Yakö indicate how profound an effect it has had on the sex ratio of the population.

---

[1]
Notes on Some Population Data from a Southern Nigerian Village, Soc. Rev.,30, 1938.

CHAPTER XIII

THE RELATIVE AGES OF SPOUSES

In the investigation of the marriages of the men of the kin group discussed in the previous chapter the positions in the age set system of both the men and women concerned were determined, and it thus became possible to analyse the relative ages of spouses.

TABLE 8   AGE-SETS OF WIVES IN RELATION TO THOSE OF HUSBANDS IN NDAI

Relation of Wives' Age Sets to Husbands':	Equivalent	Junior by:–								Senior by:–				Totals
		1	2	3	4	5	6	7	8	1	2	3	4	
Husbands' Marriages														
First	79 = 61.7%	31	6	–	–	–	–	–	–	9	2	1	–	128=100%
				37 = 28.9%								12 = 9.4%		=41.2%
Later	60 = 32.8%	49	25	7	8	4	3	2	1	15	4	4	1	183=100%
				99 = 54.1%								24 =13.1%		=58.8%
All	139 = 44.7%	80	31	7	8	4	3	2	1	24	6	5	1	311=100%
				136 = 43.7%								36= 11.6%		=100%

As is shown in Table 8 the majority (62%) of 128 first marriages of these men have been with women of an age set equivalent to their own. First marriages with women of age sets junior to those of the husbands have been only half as frequent (29%) and in nearly all these cases the wife has been only one set junior. Only 9% of first marriages have been with women of age sets senior to the husbands and in most cases the wives have been only one set senior. But of 183 later marriages of the men only a third (33%) have been with women of age sets equivalent to their own. Over half (54%) were with women of junior age sets and half of these (51%) were junior by more than one set. 13% were with women of older age sets but in the great majority of these cases the women were only one set senior. It is not impossible that in exceptional cases a woman one set junior or senior to a man may differ from him by only a few months in actual age; but in general such a woman is likely to be three or four years younger or older than the husband as the case may be, and – since one set covers a three to four year span – the difference may be as great as seven or eight years. There is, therefore, a marked tendency for young men to marry girls of their own age in the first instance and, where the wife of a first marriage is senior or junior to the husband in age set, the difference is rarely one of more than a single set while marriages with juniors are three times as common as marriages with seniors. On the other hand in later marriages some men take women who differ widely from them in age, and the general tendency is to marry younger women. So far this analysis, which is based on the marriages of men of all ages, takes no account of any possible difference in the relative ages of spouses in the case of men of various ages.

Changes in Relative Ages of Spouses. It is of considerable interest to know whether there has been any significant change during the past two generations covered by the data presented above in the relative ages of husbands and wives. The sample available is unfortunately small, as records of only 128 first marriages are available, and these are for men ranging widely in age from c.18 to over 75 years of age in 1939. The material is therefore classed into only three groups of young, middle aged and old men respectively in Table 9.

TABLE 9   The relative ages of first wives by age-sets of husbands

Age-Set of Husband	Equivalent	AGE SETS OF WIVES :-					Totals
		Junior by:- One	Two	One	Senior by:- Two	Three	
I		1					1
II		1					1
III		2					2
IV	1	5=31.3% –					1
V	4	11=68.7% 1					5
VI	6	–					6
							16=12.5% =100% (over 60 years)
VII	1	1		1		1	4
VIII	4	1	1	1		–	7
IX	–	1	–	–		1	
X	9	33=63.5% 1	12=23.0% –	3=5.8% –		–4=7.7% 10	52=40.6% =100%
XI	8	2	–	–	1	–	11
XII	10	5	–	–	–	–	15
XIII	1	1	2	–	–	–	4
							(60-30 years)
XIV	3	3	1	4			11
XV	14	2	1	–	1		18
XVI	6	35=58.3% 4	13=21.7% 1	4=6.7% 2		8=13.3% 13	60=46.9% =100%
XVII	8	4	1	1	–		14
XVIII	4	–	–	–	–		4
							(29-18 years)
All Sets	79	30	7	9	2	1	128
	=61.7%	=23.4% 37	=5.5%	12 =9.4%			100%

Among the 60 young men of sets XIV-XVIII who, being approximately between 18 and 29 years old in 1939 and having thus first married within the last twelve years, constitute nearly half the series available for analysis, there is a definite preponderance of first marriages with women equivalent in age set i.e. 58%; but 28% of first marriages were with women of junior grades and 13% with women of senior sets. Among the 52 men aged between approximately 30 and 60 years (sets XIII to VII) i.e. men who first married between approximately 12 and 42 years ago, the proportion of marriages with women of equivalent age sets was 5% higher, viz. 63% the proportion of marriages with women of junior sets remained approximately the same, viz. 29%, but those with women of senior sets were only 8% of the total. In the small surviving group of 16 men approximately 60 years of age or more (sets I to VI) i.e. men who first married 42 or more years ago - the percentage of first marriages with women equivalent in age set has risen to 69%, while the remaining 31% of first marriages were all with women of junior by only one set, there being no instances of first marriages with women senior in age set.

It may, therefore, be concluded that first marriage with a woman of age set equivalent to that of the husband i.e. with a woman differing in age from the husband by three or four years at most is an established and persistent feature of Yakö mating. The proportion of first marriages with juniors has remained at rather less than a third of all first marriages throughout the period available for study; but in no case has a first wife been more than two sets (a maximum of about ten years) junior to her husband. At the same time it is indicated that there has been an increasing tendency in the last 40 years and especially in the last ten years for men to take as first wives women of sets senior to their own, since 13% of the first marriages of the younger men and 8% of those of the middle aged men are of this character, while there is no indication of the existence of this practice among the oldest men. This tendency is obviously likely to reflect a slight but increasing dearth in the last generation of young women of equivalent age set and available as spouses for young men when the latter first reach the age of marriage.

Several possible conditions applicable to the Yakö may be involved in this increasing dearth of equivalent age set spouses for young men at their first marriages. Of these there is first the possibility of an increase in the proportion of young women who at their first marriages become second or later wives of older men. The existence of such a tendency may be sought in the data on the later marriages of men of various sets.

TABLE 10   Relative Age Sets of Spouses in (a) First and (b) Later Marriages of Ndai Men by Age Sets.

Age Sets and approximate ages of Husbands		AGE SETS OF WIVES						
		Equivalent		Junior		Senior		Totals
			%		%		%	%
I - VI (78 - 60 yrs.) (13 men)	a)	11 =	68.7	5 =	31.3	0 =	0	16 = 100
	b)	11= 32.3		22 = 64.7		1 =	3.0	34 = 100
VII - XIII (56 - 32 yrs.) (52 men)	a)	33 =	63.5	15 =	28.8	4 =	7.7	52 = 100
	b)	28= 34.1		41 = 50.0		13 = 15.9		82 = 100
XIV -XVIII (29 - 19 yrs.) (50 men)	a)	35 =	58.4	17 =	28.3	8 =	13.3	60 = 100
	b)	21= 31.3		36 = 53.7		10 = 15.0		67 = 100
All Grades (115 men)	a)	79 =	61.7	37 =	28.9	12 =	9.4	128 = 100
	b)	60= 32.8		99 = 54.1		24 = 13.1		183 = 100
a) + b)		139 =	44.7	136 =	43.7	36 =	11.6	311 = 100

Taking the age groupings used above we see from Table 10 that 13 men of 60 years or more in 1939 had married 34 later wives and that 22,or 65%, of these were junior to their husbands in age set. The 52 men between approximately 30 and 60 years of age had married 82 second or later wives of whom 41, or 50%, were junior, while 60 of the younger men, under 30 years have already married 67 second or later wives of whom 36, or 54%, were juniors. The second and particularly the third group may be held not to have completed their later marriages, but only the youngest men of sets XVII and XVIII can be regarded as likely to marry further young unmarried women in a considerable number in the future since it is rare for men to take as second wives previously unmarried women more than two classes junior than themselves and only 20 instances of this has occurred among all the 183 recorded second or later marriages of Ndai men.

Thus among the 42 men of sets XIV, XV and XVI (aged c.29 to 23 years) very few further marriages with young girls will take place. If we inspect the later marriages which these men have already made we find that they include 34 marriages with women of junior sets out of a total of 61, or 56%, a proportion intermediate between those for the groups of middle aged and old men. There is therefore evidence that the proportion of later marriages of men with women junior to them in age set has been considerable throughout the last 40 years but there is no indication that its incidence has undergone any substantial change.

While it must be recognised that by no means all the later wives of Ndai men who are junior to their husbands in age set were unmarried girls before these marriages, actually, as may be seen from Table 10, 70,or 71% of them were young unmarried girls at the time of the marriage and only 29, or 33% were widows or divorcees. This proportion implies a substantial encroachment by older already married men on the supply of women of junior age sets as they reach nubility. Given a normal sex ratio the practice of second marriages with young unmarried girls is obviously incompatible with the Yakö attitude that, as has been shown by the earlier analysis and as they themselves say, a youth should seek his first wife among unmarried girls of age sets equivalent to his own. That the sex ratio of children born in Umor and of those reaching marriageable ages is likely to be normal among the Yakö has already been pointed out. It is therefore likely that the continued practice of polygynous marriage of men with young girls is connected with the recent increase referred to above in the number of first marriages of young men with women senior to them in age set,[1] and also for the still more marked increase in the

---

[1] In only 2 of the 8 instances, however, were the wives of these first marriages divorcees: the rest had previously been unmarried; among the 4 first wives of middle aged men who were senior to their husbands only one had been previously unmarried, one was a divorcee and two were widows.

TABLE 11   The Incidence of Marriages of Ndai Men with Unmarried, Divorced and Widowed women
of Junior (J), Equivalent (E) & Senior (S) Age Sets

Rel.Age Grade of Wives	Unmarried J	E	S	Divorced J	E	S	Widows J	E	S	Totals J	E	S	Grand Total
First Marriages of Husbands	32	78	7	2	1	3	3	0	2	37	79	12	
	117			6			5			27.2%	56.8%	53.3%	128=41.2%
	=91.4%			=4.6%			=4.0%						
Later Marriages of Husbands	70	29	3	19	23	14	10	8	7	99	60	24	
	102			56			25			72.8%	43.2%	66.7%	183=58.8%
	=55.7%			=30.6%			=13.7%						
All Marriages of Husbands	102	107	10	21	24	17	13	8	9	136	139	36	
	219			62			30			100%	100%	100%	311=100%
	=70.4%			=20.0%			=9.6%						

87

proportion of women senior to their husbands in age set among the <u>later</u>
wives of the younger men. While there is only one instance of a   wife
senior in age-set among the 34 later marriages of the old men(over sixty
in 1939), such wives account for 15% of the later marriages in both the
younger groups of men. The position is even more striking than this suggests for of the total of 24 later marriages with senior women only five
were those of men of approximately 44 years or more in 1939 (sets X and
upwards), while 19, or 79%, were marriages of men approximately 25   to
40 years old. On the data available therefore later marriages   of men
with women senior to them in age set began to be frequent about   twenty
years ago, while first marriages of youths with girls senior in set became frequent still later i.e. about ten years ago, among men of sets XIV
and later, aged about 29 years or less in 1939.

As, however, it has already been shown that the proportion of later
marriages of men with women junior to them in age has not changed   substantially during the past 40 years, the practice is not likely by itself
to account for the increasing tendency of young men to marry senior women at their first marriages. It is, therefore, clearly necessary in the
first place to consider how it ever became possible to establish and maintain under conditions of apparently normal sex ratio of births the   apparently incompatible practices of first marriages of men with unmarried
girls of equivalent or junior age set and of frequent later marriages of
men with young girls junior to them in age. The feature of Yakö society
which would account both for the concurrence of these practices in the
past and for the indications of a recent change in trend has already been
referred to. This is the practice of purchasing foreign children, known
as yafoli, who are predominantly female. These acquisitions have for an
indefinite period in the past had the effect of increasing at any given
time the ratio of nubile girls to youths contracting their first   marriages and have thus made available a surplus of nubile girls for   marriage to older men as their later wives. But, as has been mentioned, there
has since British administration began in the Cross River country forty
years ago, been increasing governmental check on this trafficking in children which culminated in the early twenties when the practice was great-
ly curtailed by increased vigilance and severe penalties. In the   Ndai
patriclan in 1939 of the 11 men known to me to have purchased   foreign
children all were 36 years or more in age and most of them were over 50.
They had between them purchased 16 foreign children, of whom only one was
a male and all were said to be adult in 1939. None of the younger   men
had obtained foreign children.

The former existence of this supply of surplus female children which
has been severely curtailed during the past twenty years or so would thus
readily account for the character and changes in the relative ages of spouses
analysed above. The increase among the younger men of first marriages to
women senior to them in age including some widows and divorcees is likely

to be an effect of this curtailment which has reduced the ratio of nubile
girls to marriageable youths to more normal proportions in recent years.
At the same time it has remained customary for older men to seek   later
wives from among the nubile girls. The present position is therefore unstable and unless another external source of marriageable women is found,
which is improbable, the polygyny rate among the Yakö is likely to   decline. If the earlier situation, in which young men almost always mated
on the first occasion with previously unmarried girls, is re-established,
the later marriages of men will be fewer in number and increasingly with
divorcees and widows. If the young men compete unsuccessfully with older
men for the unmarried girls as spouses the age of first marriages of men
will tend to rise. In the earlier discussion of the increase in pre-marital pregnancy it has already been suggested that other factors may also
be tending already to raise the age of first marriage of men owing   to
difficulties in the provision of marriage money. Such difficulties   are
likely to affect older men seeking additional wives as much as or even more
than youths marrying for the first time since the former cannot so readily obtain contributions from their senior relatives for the purpose. It
is therefore most probable that, if the recent economic situation both in-
ternal and external continues substantially unchanged, the pattern of first
marriage of young men with girls marrying for the first time will persist
among the Yakö and that both the polygyny rate and the later marriage of
older men with young girls will decline.

CHAPTER XIV

FERTILITY

<u>The desire for offspring.</u> The high value set on fecundity by the Yakö is expressed and strengthened in many ways. The fertility cults,particularly those associated with the spirits of the matrilineal clans, emphasise and make explicit the sentiment that children are a blessing and a symbol of prosperity.

During the Liboku ritual at Umor when the early yams are ready for digging each year, the chief officiants led by certain of the matrilineal clan priests assemble for a preparatory rite in which the prayer is:-

Yasi odö aiyo-kokö noyo dji lidjofi
Onen woyom obö yanena totö kefat oman wen otumo
Atewa nan lose amon noyo dji lidjofi
Onen wotö kutan tobö

Today is the day before kökö (when) we will eat new yams
Anyone who lies with a woman, let her conceive and bear a child alive
Atewa! (matrilineal clan spirit) accept (this) offering (and) we will eat new yams
Anyone who has a witch let him die.

Similarly during the succeeding rite at the shrine of the premier matrilineal clan spirit Ödjokobi the appeal spoken by the priest is:

Amon noyo dji lidjofi
Letu mon lenö lepömi
Wotö lifae amon
Onen tomana ötumo

We shall eat new yams
Our head (let it be) without pain
Ourselves (let us be) in health
Anyone (born, let him) be born alive.

And in the prayer of the village speaker (Okpebri) occurs the phrase:
Obot obi: mwo öbi yanen taya mana yatumö, yasu susu

The village head says: he says people should be born strong, many many.

Similar appeals are made during the Harvest Ritual at each of the matriclan shrines when these are visited by the assembled matriclan priests during the gathering of the main yam harvest.

The most frequent of the minor rituals in a Yakö village are supplications at the innumerable shrines of minor spirits (ndet, sing. edet) on behalf of women who have so far failed to bear thriving children. For every patrilineage there is one or more of these shrines and to some of them offerings are made only for the purpose of securing fertility. New spirits are introduced quite often by enterprising men who buy the paraphernalia and instructions for the ritual from neighbouring peoples. Such a shrine begins as a means of command over supernatural benefits and as a source of profit and prestige to its 'owner'. Succession to control of the ritual is usually patrilineal, as a rule a son succeeds his father, and gradually the shrine comes to be regarded as the abode of a tutelary fertility and health giving spirit for the entire patrilineage or clan to which its introducer belonged.

Within both the patrilineal and the matrilineal clans and still more within their component lineages there is a strong sentiment that increase in numerical strength is both desirable in itself and a means of attaining relative prestige. The men of the patrilineage take pride for example in the number and size of forest lands that they and their forbears have opened up and cleared for farming, and a large and growing lineage will compare itself favourably with its smaller fellows. Need for expansion of farming land is considered a source of pride not of embarrassment. When for instance men of the Itewa lineage of Ndai-Lekpangkem patriclan in Umor recently found themselves in need of more land it was with pride that a deputation headed by their path-elder went to seek the concurrence of Ngkpani village in the clearing of a tract in the forest which lies between the farmed areas of Umor and Ngkpani. Taking a gift to the village head of Ngkpani they explained why new farmland was needed as a result of an increase in the number of their young men. Later these Itewa men, whom a few men of another lineage joined, sought the aid of the Obot Kepün of Ndai-Lekpangkem who called upon all men of the patriclan to go with them to help clear the forest growth, and in fact a very large part of the adult male strength of the clan mustered on the site to give this aid to their fellows who were extending their farmlands. The tone of the accounts I was given of this particular expansion undoubtedly implied a sense of worthiness and self-congratulation on the part of the Itewa men and of general satisfaction in the patriclan as a whole. There was recurrent emphasis on its growing strength. This same patriclan whose dwelling area is situated in the interior of the village and is circumscribed by those of neighbouring clans, also established during the interval between my two visits a new outlying settlement area or kowu (pl. liwu) in a stretch of their former farming land on the outskirts of the village. The congestion in the main settlement area to which this move was due was similarly looked upon not as a nuisance or misfortune but on the contrary as a result of welcome growth of the clan. To have established a kowu as many of the patriclans of Umor have done in the past fifty years is also a source of pride.

Within the patriclan (kepŭn) the group sentiment for fertility   is
fostered by the desire that fathers should have many sons to succeed them
in their compounds and on their farms. The matriclans (yajima) are not
territorially compact groups but the complementary sentiment, the desire
for the fertility of their women who are scattered as wives through   the
patriclan of the village is equally strong. A man looks to his sisters to
provide him with heirs, men who will belong to his matrilineage and succeed to his property, and to satisfy the desire for many children that is
so frequently expressed in supplications to the shrines of the matriclans.

Consonant with this emphasis on fertility is the exaction of penalties for abortion. Abortion is said to be rarely attempted by the   Yakö
although they claim to know effective abortifacents. In this context the
point of interest is that abortion is regarded as an offence against the
spirit of the woman's matriclan which endangers the wellbeing of all members of the group. An alleged abortion should be investigated by the village head and his council of Yabot and, if it is considered proven,   the
close matrikin relatives of the offending women are required to provide a
cow which is ceremonially butchered and consumed by the Yabot, which includes all the matriclan priests, in the course of an offering at   the
shrine of the woman's clan. Cattle, of the dwarf forest breed, are   not
numerous among the Yakö and in recent times a sum of several pounds contributed by most members of the woman's matrilineage would be required to
provide the beast. The enforcement of this penalty, which is one reserved for grave offences, is assured if necessary by refusing access to the
shrine of the clan spirit for any ritual until the cow has been   handed
over. I did not obtain an account of a recent instance of this legal process which is perhaps rarely carried out, since discovery of abortion is
by no means easy, but there is undoubtedly among the Yakö a strong sentiment that abortion is an offence calculated to involve supernatural punishment of the culprit and her matri-kinsfolk if the clan spirit be not
appeased.

But, while the Yakö seek by both practical and ritual means to promote childbirth, its frequency is at the same time restricted by a   pro-
hibition of sexual intercourse to nursing mothers. Within a few days of
bearing a child most Yakö women resume domestic and even farm work,   but
for two years the child is suckled by the mother, although it is given
cooked yam within a few months of birth and after the first year is also
fed with portions of practically every dish that is prepared. During those
two years the mother should refrain from sexual intercourse. This   pro-
hibition is upheld by the Yakö not on physiological grounds such as that,
for instance, another pregnancy by ending the mother's flow of milk would
endanger the earlier child, but in the belief that the act of coitus itself would cause the child to sicken. This effect is not associated with
the action of any particular supernatural agency. When I sought further
explanations I was told on several occasions that it simply was so.   The

rule is, however, very generally respected and it is believed coitus interruptus during this period is dangerous. Nevertheless intercourse does admittedly occur quite often before a child is weaned and several men insisted on several occasions that the wives and not men who were usually responsible for the breach. Desire or jealousy often lead the wife to make the indirect advances which are all that a Yakö woman may ever decently employ when seeking her husband's embraces. That the urge to break the rule should come from the wife is understandable in terms of Yakö mating for a young husband may find a lover among the unmarried girls while an older man is likely to have a second wife who is not suckling a child and is free to receive him. I encountered a few instances of a woman bearing two live children within a period of two years but was told that this was very unusual, and on the whole I am inclined to believe that this ban on intercourse during lactation is nearly always maintained for the first year or perhaps longer, but that sexual relations are frequently resumed before the entire period of two years elapsed.

The high value set on fecundity is also set aside when twins are born. In the native view, which is but slowly being affected by the efforts of mission and administration to preserve and safeguard them, twins should never be put to the mother's breast but be taken to the bush in the night and buried there. The birth of twins is considered to be due to an offence on the part of the mother. It may result, for example, from adultery during pregnancy and in Umor it is regarded as a supernatural punishment by Keta, the tutelary spirit of men which is impersonated in a secret ritual by the head of a society into which all males are initiated in youth. Keta may be invoked against any woman who acts maliciously towards a man.

Actual Fertility. In order to determine the natural fertility of Yakö women an attempt was made to investigate the reproductive histories of a number of women who had completed the reproductive period in 1939. For this purpose women of age set IX or senior i.e. who were approximately 48 or more years old in 1939 were selected. The number obtainable for study among the wives of men of the Ndai patriclan 42 in all, was unfortunately small but the results, which are summarised in the following table, are fully consistent with the particulars of the reproductive histories down to 1939 of a larger sample of 210 women.

TABLE 12   Children born to Ndai wives who have completed the reproductive
period *

Number of Mothers			42
Number of live births	male	66	
	female	58	
	Total		124

Mean number of live births	both sexes	...	2.95
" " " " "	females	...	1.38

Number of miscarriages and still births †	11
Mean number of " " " "	0.26

Number of surviving offspring:

	Male	Female	Total
Adults	38	41	79
Minors ‡	8	3	11
	46	44	90

Mean number of surviving offspring	...	2.15
" " " " females	...	1.05

The frequencies of births among the 42 women were as follows:-

(i) Frequency of numbers of live births

Births	Cases
1 ·	7
2	9
3	12 ·
4	9
5	3
6	2
	42

* Women of age-sets IX or senior i.e. aged 48 years or more in 1939.
† This number was difficult to check and some cases may have been omitted.
‡ Unmarried girls, boys and youths.

(ii) Frequency of numbers of surviving offspring

Births	Cases
0	2
1	13
2	13
3	7
4	5
5	2
	42

(iii) Frequency of numbers of live female births

Female Births	Cases
0	9
1	19
2	8
3	3
4	1
5	2
	42

(iv) Frequency of numbers of surviving female offspring

Female Survivors	Cases
0	13
1	21
2	4
3	2
4	1
5	1
	42

If this random sample, small though it is, be accepted as representative for the Yakö, apart from the fact that it includes no case of a bar-
ren woman, it would appear that the mean number of births per wife is 3
(2.95). that only one third of the women bear more than three live children during their entire reproductive period and that five or more   live
births are very exceptional. The frequency of miscarriages and still births
is high and the mortality of offspring is also high.

This sample gives the general impression of low effective fertility. The mean number of surviving female offspring of women who have completed the reproductive period is 1.05. This figure will lie between the gross and net reproductive rates for women. It is less than the gross rate(1.38) because some of the daughters born to these women have already died and higher than the net rate since some of those still living will themselves die before completing their reproductive life. We know that of the 58 live born daughters of these women 14 or 24% had already died by 1939 so that at least a quarter of the female offspring of these women who have completed the reproductive period will have died before they in turn have completed their reproductive life. Assuming a total loss by the age of fifty of 27% on the gross rate of 1.38 live female births per woman the number of female offspring who will complete the reproductive period born to women who have themselves completed it will be approximately unity (1.007). This suggests that if, as there is no reason to doubt, the crude birth rate has been stable the net female reproduction rates over the past half century have been barely adequate to maintain the population.

This conclusion would at first sight appear to conflict with the result of an analysis of earlier data from Umor in which it was concluded that "in this population during a part at least of the (past)fifty years.. fertility and mortality have been such as to allow of a rapidly increasing population."[1] For that study the data available were particulars of the living children of the 112 living adult males of the Ndai patriclan. From this it was found first that the percentage of minors in the male population was 57% at a theshold of approximately 18 years. Since the minor/adult ratio has been found to be closely related to reproduction rates and 45% of minors at a threshold of twenty years is, in other populations, associated with a high net reproduction rate it appeared that effective fertility over the past 18 years had been high. This was supported by an estimate of 1.9 to 2.2. living male offspring reaching sixty years of age period per man who has himself reached that age, which could be considered as "an approximation to the end result of the net reproduction rates prevailing for the previous fifty years."[2]

Is this apparent discrepancy to be ascribed to the smallness of the samples which must in consequence be regarded as inadequate as a foundation for any inferences concerning fertility and the trends of population among the Yakö ? The samples are admittedly small and the results of their analysis must be considered approximate and tentative, but it can be

---

[1] Charles & Forde, Notes on Some Population Data from a Southern Nigerian Village, Soc. Rev., 30, 1939, p.10.

[2] op. cit. p.10.

shown that they do not in fact conflict and that larger samples would be likely to lead to similar results. The first point to observe is that in the sample investigated in 1935, 109 males had 187 wives and, if the further three fully adult men without wives are included we have a ratio of 1.67 wives per man. The same group when investigated in 1939 included 121 husbands who had 210 living wives and there were ten fully adult widowers and bachelors. This gives a ratio of 1.62 wives per man.

This excess of wives was not due to abnormality of sex ratio at birth among the Yakö. The data obtained both in 1935 and in 1939 indicated that the sex ratio of children born in Umor was likely to approximate to normal at birth and in later years. Thus the 1935 data gave a ratio of 102.6 females to 100 males born to Ndai men; and among the living children both adult and minor of these men, where the effect of greater age of some members would tend to increase the proportion of females, these were 201 females to 189 males, or 106.3 females to 100 males.

Given a ratio of the order of 165 wives to 100 men and a normal sex ratio of births a situation in which the women completing the reproductive period are replaced at the rate of 1.0 while men over sixty years of age are replaced at a rate of approximately 2.0 is no longer anomalous. There may be a somewhat slightly greater increase of mortality among males with increasing age but we may assume broadly that for every female born who lives to old age a male does the same. Since there are 165 females in the population for every 100 males it is clear that while the birth of 165 surviving males would result in a considerable excess over replacement of the 100 males the birth of an equivalent number of surviving females would merely replace the 165 females and give no such excess.[1]

The main source of the excess of wives among the Yakö has been indicated in an earlier section. It is due to the acquisition of foreign female children and we are again, in the fertility data considered here confronted with the effects of this formerly extensive practice of obtaining foreign infants who are given status as children in the households and

---

[1] The ratio of men to wives viz. 1:1.65 does not correspond exactly to the ratio between the estimated replacement rates of men and women viz.1:2; but exact correspondence is not to be expected. The ratio of men to wives includes adults of all ages while the replacement rates have been estimated for men at c.60 years and for women at c.50 years and in the absence of mortality rates at various ages it is not possible to estimate closely what the ratio of men of sixty years to wives of fifty years would be. Furthermore the ratio of men to wives in recent years will be dependent not only on the replacement rates during the past fifty years but also on the ratio of men to wives which existed at the beginning of that period.

clans of their purchasers. The combination of a high rate of natural increase of the male population with only moderate fertility of women may,
therefore, be regarded as a result of the artificial increase in the number of females by the accession during childhood of females from   other
populations and the high incidence of polygyny that this has made possible. It has resulted in a high increase in population of which there is
also abundant evidence in the expansion of the occupied area of the Umor
village site during the past two or three generations. But, as has been
pointed out earlier, it is a factor which is ceasing to operate at   the
present time and if natural fertility remains unchanged the rate   of
growth of population, like the incidence of polygyny, may be expected to
fall off sharply in the immediate future.

CHAPTER XV

HOUSEHOLD AND FAMILY

When the first wife of a Yakö comes to live in the woman's house he has provided for her in the dwelling area of his patriclan a new household is created and so long as she remains with her husband the wife participates in its maintenance. General features of domestic activities and the respective contributions of husband and wife to the common effort have already been indicated in the earlier sections, but some of the consequent relations between husband and wife will be considered here in greater detail. It has been shown that where there is polygyny every wife has a right to occupy a separate house provided by her husband and has personal property in food supplies and domestic equipment. She has the right   to rear her own children and engage in both productive and recreational activities free from the interference of any other wife. A man with his several wives normally constitutes a single farming unit, but here again each wife has her specific interests, rights and duties which do not   extend over the entire farm plot and one wife does not control the farm labour of the others.

Multiple Households. The term 'polygynous household' which is often applied to such a situation does not therefore correctly suggest the domestic conditions of polygyny among the Yakö. In polygyny here we   have strictly speaking a number of households which have a single household head in common. The close proximity of the houses of plural wives   and their common concern with the affairs of one husband undoubtedly lead to mutual personal relations between the wives but these are informal in character. They depend on individual temperament and according to the particular circumstances may be relations of companionship and protection on the one hand or of jealousy and hostility on the other. The important sociological point is that these attitudes are not determined in   advance either by rules of domestic co-operation or of relative status of wives. The first married or the senior existing wife has no formal superiority or prerogative. In the native view, each wife has an equal claim on the time, attention and energy of the husband. Similarly each wife has an equal obligation to participate in household duties including especially farmwork and preparing food for the husband, and is responsible for the wellbeing of her own children. In practice, owing to differences in the aptitudes and inclinations of wives and in the sentiments of the husband towards his wives, there may be considerable differences between them both in their participations in domestic activities and in their prestige in the   compound. But such differences are not subject to the control of the senior wife. On the farm it is the husband who tells each wife what he   wishes her to do. A Yakö farm is planted in sections, each section being an area cleared at one time by a clearing party of men at the opening of the farming year. A man with two or more wives, who is likely to have had his farm cleared in half a dozen or more sections, will indicate to each wife the sections in which she is to make yam hills, plant her secondary crops of maize, beans and so forth and work throughout the period of cultivation. He will also control the planting of her yams.

Wives differ in their interests in oil palm preparation and in petty trading of vegetable products such as coco-yams, 'spinach', okra cooked beans etc., in the village markets. It may be found that plural wives have settled down to some degree of specialisation in these activities. Mutual helpfulness between wives in farming and domestic activities is by no means absent among the Yakö, but at the same time it is quite common to find an age mate of one wife helping her in some task at home or in the farm while the other wife is working independently. The relations between the wives of one man may range from real companionship to a minimum of contact punctuated with outbursts of hostility. The failure of one wife to live amicably with another in the compound is indeed a recognised ground for dismissing the aggressor and several instances of divorce for this reason were known to me in Umor. It was usually, but not always the later married wife who was dismissed in this way.

There is similarly no fixed opinion among the Yakö concerning the relative desirability of becoming a first or a later wife. It is probable that the majority of young girls prefer to wed youths who are marrying for the first time, but this appears to be associated rather with youthful pleasures of courtship and the claim at that time on the exclusive attention of the bridegroom than with any conventional or personal attitude to post-marital status. It must also be borne in mind that a man's later wives may, since they are often divorcees or widows, be junior only in order of marriage and not in age set or years. To be a man's first wife by no means implies that a woman will always be the senior in age and the most experienced woman in the compound.

Furthermore the domestic units directly related to one man may include those of not only his wives but also divorced or widowed kinswomen among whom mother, sisters and sisters' daughters are the most frequently encountered. A woman widowed late in life usually joins the household of one of her sons in whose farm she will plant her crops. A younger woman who has been widowed or divorced may temporarily rejoin the household of her parents or go to her mother's brother or a brother. Such women are provided with houses of their own and unless they are infirm provide their own food supplies. Their rights and obligations to the household head are in many respects, particularly those concerned with farming and domestic supplies, similar to those of the wives and any young children with them will be regarded as his foster-sons and daughters. Elderly widowers are also to be found as dependents in the households of one of their sons; while men who are mental or physical defectives usually go to live after their father's deaths with one of their brothers. There are also in many

Yakö households young children related to only one of the spouses whose origins and subsequent status will be considered later.

Since a short term is required to refer to a domestic group of this kind resulting mainly from polygyny but also including dependent kinswomen and their offspring it may be called a multiple household.

Domestic Obligations. The domestic arrangements of the Yakö appeared to me very variable. I did not obtain sufficient case material to make statistical analysis possible and can only indicate the varieties of domestic behaviour which emerge from my scattered records of particular households. The majority of men provide themselves with a separate man's house, usually a smaller and simpler dwelling than a woman's in which they keep belongings, meet their friends, rest and often sleep. For the first years of marriage young men frequently dispense with this privacy which of course entails extra effort in housebuilding. Often, too, young men will share the house of a father, elder brother or other relative living in the same compound, but it is general for men in their thirties to build themselves a man's house. On the other hand I encountered instances of men of late middle age who lived and kept their goods entirely in a wife's house. Some of these men had considerable standing, one was a priest-chief, and would have had no difficulty in securing the materials and assistance needed for building a separate house. My impression was that all such men were monogamists, but I did not pursue the point systematically enough to establish this.

There are no rigid standards of domestic eating among the Yakö. A man may come to eat in his wife's house and take his food at the same time as the wife and children. On the other food will at his request be carried to him in his man's house and this is usually done for the main meal of the day, at sundown, if the husband has with him other men, one or two companions who have helped him in a farm task or a visitor from another village for example, to whom he also wishes to offer food. In a multiple household there is likewise no fixed practice whereby the various wives provide food for the husband. Each wife feeds herself and her dependents. Indeed from the point of view of daily food supply there are as many households as there are adult able bodied women. Food should be provided for the husband by each wife in turn, but the length and regularity of the periods appear to be very variable. Some men receive food for a week, from one kokö to the next, from each wife; others may change from day to day. Some husbands are punctilious, others are casual. Not infrequently a man will cook food for himself either in a wife's house when she is away from home or in his own house, for every man can roast and boil yams and make an oil and meat stew. Some men pride themselves on their skill as cooks and the meat at feasts is usually cooked by men. The pounding of fufu alone is regarded as exclusively a woman's task.

A husband expects his wife to see to the maintenance of her own food supplies and household needs. He never carries wood and water and, although it is left to the wife to provide the seed and undertake all the work of cultivating and preserving the secondary crops such as corn, dried okra, beans, spinach and the indispensible peppers which are much valued as ingredients in Yakö dishes, a man is considered justifiably irate if his wife fails to maintain adequate supplies. If a wife is for any reason unable to carry out all the farm work that falls to her lot and may reasonably be expected it is for her to find and recompense helpers from among her age mates or her matrilineal kin.

If a wife lacks sufficient yams to supply her share for the needs of her husband and children she is expected to work on other people's farms at busy times and especially at planting and harvesting when she will be given yams for each day's work which may remedy her own deficit. A husband with a large harvest of yams will himself give a wife extra yams in recognition of her farming services to him if her own crop is short; but I found in a detailed investigation of farm labour and supplies that the women with few yams are nearly always wives of men who also have harvests which are insufficient for household needs. In such circumstances it is the wife who makes up the balance by her work on the farms of others, particularly of matrilineal relatives and of her own age mates.

Adultery   A wife can place no legal restriction on the sexual activities of her husband, but he is entitled to claim monetary compensation from a man with whom she has committed adultery, to divorce her and receive back the marriage money. In practice, as has been noted, a wife is rarely divorced unless her adultery is persistent, but compensation for adultery is frequently secured and is now recognised by the Native Court. Sums up to two pounds have been awarded in recent years.

Adultery of a wife with a patriclansman of her husband is regarded more seriously than adultery outside the patriclan. It has an incestuous character which requires ritual expiation in relation to the clan group in addition to compensation to the injured husband and is an offence which may be held to disqualify a man from performance of clan rituals. In one patriclan of Umor the assistant ('palm wine pourer') to the clan priest head (Obot Kepun) was held to have committed adultery with a fellow clansman's wife. After a long and acriminous dispute he paid one pound ten shillings as compensation to the injured husband and provided a goat for an offering at the clan shrine (epundet) in which all the elders took part. The elders of several lineages insisted that he could no longer act as assistant to the clan head, but were not able to get their way. When however the head died some years later the dispute flared up again. In the ordinary way the assistant succeeds as priest head but there was intense opposition to this among the most of the elders and the head of another lineage was put forward as successor. At this time a young pregnant woman of the patriclan who belonged to the lineage of the assistant priest was waiting for the performance of the 'navel putting' rite at the clan shrine. With the connivance of her father and elders of the lineage the assistant priest performed the rite without letting others know in advance of his intentions. The other elders were furious and a serious quarrel began which might have ended in clan fission by the secession of the lineage of the assistant priest. Within a few days however the assistant himself fell ill and he died shortly after. His death so soon after this act created a profound impression both in the clan and in the village at large for it was generally accepted as a punishment of sacrilege by the patriclan spirit.

Men sometimes receive women other than their wives in their house at night. Whether such a liaison be adulterous or not neither the wives nor the patriclan fellows of the man will usually interfere unless the relation is incestuous and intervention by a wife's kinsfolk would not be considered justified if the husband beat her for exposing a clandestine relation with another woman. A wife may attempt to curb extra-marital sexual relations on her husband's part by jealous behaviour, and complaints to her matrilineal kin that she is neglected, but such a complaint may equally well be made in respect of the husband's relations with another wife or wives.

<u>Companionship between Spouses.</u> Outside the woman's house and to a less extent the farm a Yakö man and wife are rarely found together as companions. Not only are men and wives separated in their memberships of economic groups such as age set path clearing parties and farm working parties, as well as of esoteric ritual groups including secret societies,but they also tend to remain apart in both ceremonial and recreational activities. It has been seen that the Yakö wedding feasts are actually feasts given by the bride's father to his friends and by her mother to hers, not joint feasts given by the parents to mutual friends of both sexes. A similar alignment is found in Yakö funerary ritual. There is, as was illustrated in the account of Yakö marriage ritual, co-operation between men and wives in ceremonial activities but they do not constitute a couple in relation to others.

This separation extends to minor economic activities even to those of a strictly household character. Thus it is very unusual to see a Yakö man and wife walking together on a bush path to their farm. Wives go alone or in parties of neighbouring women; husbands likewise go independently or with their friends. In the farm itself each is usually engaged in separate tasks sometimes with the aid of friends of the same sex. In the preparation of oil palm products husbands and wives each carry out separate customary operations; a husband will get one or more age mates or youths of his patriclan,but not his wife, to help him pound fruits in the great log mortar. He on the other hand does not take part in boiling the

fruit or skimming the oil, while cracking nuts to extract kernels   is   a
women's task and the kernels are the wife's reward for her share in   the
work.

There are however exceptions both to the customary division of household activities between men and wives and also to the general principle of
separation between spouses itself. In Umor one oldish man whom I knew well
was almost inseparable from his wife on domestic occasions, I would meet
them together on the farm path and on his frequent visits to me his wife
nearly always accompanied him. He was a benign, vague and rather   inef-
fectual person, clearly dependent on his younger and more vigorous wife.
I also noted other instances from time to time of unaccustomed companionship of man and wife. Women may also on occasion participate in a ritual
in virtue of their being the wife of the priest or of another officient.
Thus during the Lebokū rites of 1939 the wife of the village head on several occasions entered the Odjokobi shrine housed in his compound after
he and the other priests had carried out a ritual so that she too might
be smeared with the sacred chalk. On one occasion she brought her children with her. No other women participated and subsequent questioning made
it clear that it was by favour of the priests because she was a wife of
the village head that she obtained the blessing of the fertility spirit
of her husband's matrilineal clan. Nevertheless it remains true   that
there is by custom a high degree of separation between the activities of
man and wife which restricts companionship between them largely to leisure
hours in the house. Man and wife are rarely seen together in public and
their wider social activities are found in distinct and indeed mutually exclusive groups.

On the other hand common interests and complementary activities in
the household do afford spouses ample occasion for the growth of affection, for the expression of esteem and also for dispute. To the outsider
the latter are the more obstrusive and the alleged reasons for domestic
quarrels between men and wives are very various. They range from disputes concerning the treatment of children, the provision of food and of
oil palm fruits to charges of witchcraft and of adultery.

Foster-Parentage and Adoption. As has already been pointed out there
are very frequently in Yako households minors other than children of the
man by his wife. Such minors may include sons and daughters of the man
or his wife by previous marriages, children of widowed or divorced relatives, usually brothers or sisters of either the man or his wife and until recently there were foreign children purchased by the man or more
rarely his wife. A census of the households of over 100 men with nearly
200 wives made in 1935 in the dwelling area of the Ndai patriclan showed
that among these foster-children sons and daughters of the wives by former husbands from whom they had been divorced were the most numerous class.

Of the 382 children in Ndai (187 boys and 195 girls) no fewer than 113 (55 boys and 58 girls) or about 30% were not children born to the men in whose households they were living. On the other hand 43 of the children born to Ndai men were not living in their fathers households. Of the 113 introduced children 57 or almost exactly half were **children** of the wives by previous husbands and over 70% of these were girls. Thus the most common foster-parent is the step-father - a later husband of a divorced woman or widow. The other foster-children fell into two groups, the larger consisted of 37 who were matrilineal or more rarely patrilineal kin of the man and of these nearly all i.e. 33, were boys; while the remaining 19 children were kin of the wife's of whom the majority (13) were girls. Of the boys who were the man's kin most were brothers' or sister's sons. The former, since they had come to the household of their father's brothers, were still living in the dwelling area of their patriclan of birth and no question of their patrilineal clan affiliation would arise when they became adult. The sisters' sons on the other hand were foster-children in patriclans other than those of their fathers.

In the households of 109 men there were only 9 children by deceased or divorced wives living with their fathers, and all of them were boys, while there were 43 children living away with absent mothers or their kin.

This distribution of foster-children in consequence of the death or divorce of parents is affected by several divergent attitudes concerning both the immediate needs and the ultimate status of the children. When a mother is divorced very young children nearly always go with her and remain in her care in her new home. If a mother dies her young children may be brought up by other wives of their father or by relatives of either the father or the deceased mother. The immediate welfare of the child and the need for a woman to look after it are paramount. No particular domicile is prescribed. With older children the attitude towards the custody of boys and girls differs. A father usually makes little attempt to keep young daughters in his household; they usually accompany a divorced mother, but he will usually maintain his paternal right to receive the marriage money when in due course the daughter marries. But the foster-father particularly if he is the mother's brother may replace the father and receive the marriage money if the father does not assert his right. On the other hand a father often retains in his household a son who is more than four or five years old when the mother dies or is divorced. If a divorced wife attempts to secure custody of a son against the father's will the latter can enforce his right by appeal to the ward or village head. If he agrees that his son shall accompany his mother or be fostered by a mother's brother he does not thereby consent to the adoption of the son into the patrilineal kin group of its mother's brother or still less of her later husband and he can require the return of a son to his own household later in childhood. The retention of young children in the household of the father after the departure or death of the mother is, however, rare among the Yako and in the households investigated occurred in only one case in six.

But the high incidence of foster-parentage which this implies under conditions of frequent divorce must not be taken to indicate an equal frequency of adoption. Adoption is to be distinguished from foster-parentage; the latter implies a change in household membership during minority but not of patri-clan affiliation; adoption does not affect household membership but implies a change in residence and patriclan affiliation when adult. A foster-child is one who is passing some of the years of minority in a household other than that of its father. Such a child continues to be regarded as a member of the patriclan of its father i.e. the husband of its mother at the time of its birth while an adoptee (owunen) is one whose patrilineal affiliation is transferred from the clan of his father to that of his adopter. Among the Yakö foster-parentage and adoption are successive situations in the sense that adoption may follow foster-childhood, but cannot exist simultaneously, for adoption cannot be said to exist until the point at which the adoptee enters on adult life with the establishment of a separate household. Foster-childhood on the other hand can be a condition only of minors.

While adoption frequently follows foster-childhood and may justly be regarded as a likely consequence of it, it does not necessarily follow and may occur without precedent foster-childhood. The native attitude on the connection between fostering and the assumption of parental obligations is indicated by the following native statement: "If you live with one of your relatives from boyhood to the age of marriage that relative of yours will marry the first wife for you with payment in full. When you start a farm he will give you a share of yams from his stack and show a plot to plant in, and a place in the yam stack to tie your sticks of yams and a place in the bush with palm trees to collect palm fruits and tap palm wine and pear trees of his from which you can take the fruits. He will help to build you a fine house in his kepun dwelling area. That is why you have to be specially full of respect to that relative. Most men are doing this although some do not."

Thus adoption is in practice established by the provision by the foster-parent of marriage money, house site and farming land. A father, or, if he has died, the patrilineal kinsman who stands in his place, will usually maintain contact with a youth who is foster-child to another and encourage his return at manhood to the patriclan of his birth. It is only when as a child he has been entrusted to his mother's brother, which would require the father's consent, that he is likely to associate himself permanently with the patriclan of his foster-father. If such is the case and the foster-father provides the greater part of the marriage payment, a house or a house site in his clan dwelling area and arranges for a plot in his clan land to be provided for the first farm, then the youth is regarded as adopted into the patriclan of that man and ranks as

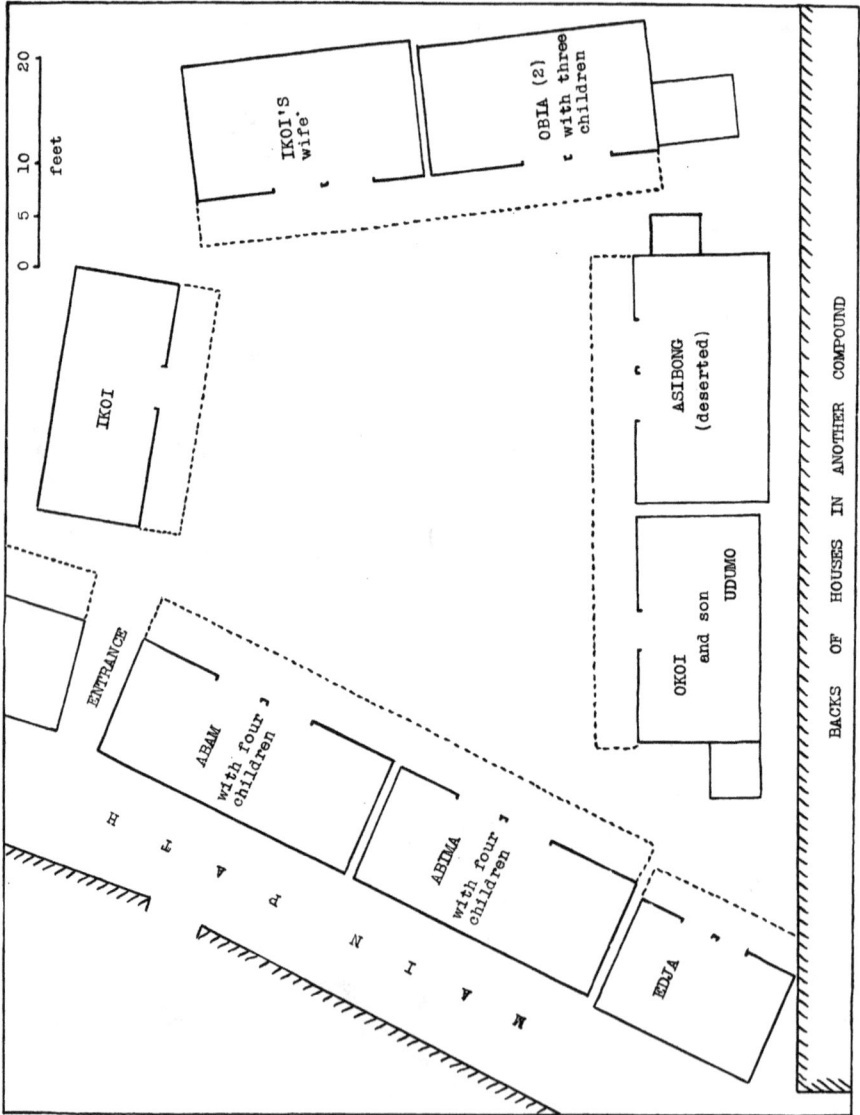

Fig. 3. The Compound of Okoi in 1935.

his son. It may occasionally happen that a mother's brother or more rarely a step-father will provide the greater part of the marriage payment, if the youth lacks a father or other patrilineal relative who has the means to do so, without seeking adoption of the youth, who will then reside with his father's patriclansmen and farm with them. Adoption changes the patriclan affiliation of a man and his descendants but never the matrilineal affiliation to which the provision of marriage money, place of residence and farming lands is irrelevant.

A man may be adopted later in adult life in circumstances which have been discussed elsewhere; and here again the transfer is essentially one of patriclan affiliation with which are associated residence and rights to farm land. Adoption among the Yakö is phrased personally and there is always a particular adopter or sponsor who replaces the father but it consists essentially in the replacement of status in one patrilineal kin group by equivalent status in another.

Adoption does not exist in the same sense for females for the patrilineal clan affiliation of a woman is of little significance after marriage. Her married life is passed in the dwelling area and on the farmlands of her husband's patriclan, while it is not her father but her mother's brother who is mainly concerned for the stability of her marriage. The father of a girl, may, as has been seen, claim to receive the payment from her spouse at her first marriage, although she has passed her infancy in the household of a foster-father. The only sense in which adoption of females may be said to occur is when the father fails to do this and the payment is received in the first place by a foster-parent who is likely to be a step-father or a mother's brother. But in fact since her patrilineal clan affiliation has little influence on her social life and is not transmitted to her children the question of transfer of patriclan affiliation does not arise, and adoption, in the sense of recognised transfer of clan affiliation, does not occur.

A Household History. The complexity and heterogeneous character of the larger Yakö households consequent on the vicissitudes of polygyny, death, divorce and foster-parentage may be illustrated from the domestic history of a man of age set VIII who in 1935 at the age of about forty-eight was head of a large household, had married nine times and at that time had four wives living with him (see fig.3).

In the compound of this man, Okoi, in Ukpakapi ward there were eight houses built round an open space about fifty feet square; those of Okoi and his wives occupied most of the three sides. Ūdūmō (age set XVII) a young adult son and the only surviving child of Okoi's first wife who left him several years ago shared, and kept his belongings in, Okoi's own man's house. Ūdumo's marriage payment had just been made and his bride, who was pregnant, was still living with her parents. She was expected to come to a woman's house in Okoi's compound in the coming year while Udumo would continue to share his father's house. For the two years before his marriage Udumo had helped his father a good deal in the farm and had collected palm fruits for him. But he had also worked for his intended father-in-law in the clearing and planting season and had brought him the customary gifts.

Abam, (age set X), the senior wife then living with Okoi, who was two age sets junior to him and about forty years old, lived in the first house on Okoi's side of the compound. She had come from an adjacent patriclan in Ukpakapi ward after the birth of her first child over twenty years previously, when she was sixteen or seventeen. She had in 1935 three young sons. Two other boys and two girls had died in infancy and her youngest child was four or five years old. She also looked after a youth of about sixteen, a foster-child who belonged to Okoi's matrilineage and had passed into his care some years ago when the boy's mother died.

Abam had Okoi's confidence in day to day affairs of the compound and farm, and regularly provided Udumo with food. Her undoubted prestige in the compound was due to her capacity and sense of responsibility rather than to formal seniority in marriage. Two of the later wives of Okoi were in fact of the same age set as Abam. She was a strong and energetic woman and cared for a large part of Okoi's farm plots. Her own personal yam harvest was larger than that of the other wives and in 1935 she had twenty sticks of yams at the main harvest.

Beyond Abam's house was that of Abima, also about forty years old (age set X), whom Okoi brought to his compound about nine years before. She had left a former husband to join Okoi and brought with her a son who was eleven or twelve years old in 1935 and lived in her house together with the three children, two girls and a boy, that she has borne to Okoi.

In the next house, a small woman's house tucked away in the corner, Edja, of about the same age (age set X) lived alone. Okoi had married her only two years previously. She too had left a former husband to join him but had disappointed Okoi both in children and in the farm. Okoi's latest wife, Obia (2),[1] (age set XII) who had joined him only a few months before, had a house on the opposite side of the compound. Some time before she came to Okoi she had left a former husband, who was said to have been a neglectful farmer who did not give her yams enough for the household, and had been living with her own mother. When she came to Okoi, Obia (2) brought her two infant daughters with her while her son by her

---

[1] Indicated thus as an earlier deceased wife of Okoi, to be referred to later, was also named Obia.

first marriage had remained with another wife of his father. She was pregnant by Okoi when she came to his compound, but the child was born dead soon after. With Obia (2) lived a small son of Okoi by an earlier wife, Isu, who had left him, taking two other younger boys with her, about three years previously. Like Edja, Obia (2) had not yet borne Okoi a surviving child, but she worked well on the farm and got on well with Abam. Okoi was still disputing with Obia's matrilineal relatives and former husband over the question of marriage money. He claimed that since she was not young and had borne three children to her former husband, there was no obligation to return his marriage payment and also that after she had left her former husband she lived for nearly a year in her father's compound during which time he had made no real effort to secure her return.

Between Okoi's house and that of Obia (2) there was an empty woman's house. This had been occupied until a year before by an earlier wife, Asibong, who had joined Okoi some fourteen years earlier. The only child she bore him died, and she left Okoi after frequent quarrels in which she accuses him of neglecting her and concerning himself only with Abam and Abima. She went to live with her brother, planting her yams in his farm, but Okoi was willing and even anxious that she should return and her house stood empty, clean and in good repair. He had refused to give it to Obia (2) for whom he had just put a new roof on the old house he provided.

Besides those in the compound there were other children of Okoi who lived elsewhere. A married daughter, the only surviving child of his long divorced second wife, Okwa, had gone three years previously to join her husband. Before that she had been looked after by Abam, but since marriage had not often come to the compound.

Okoi also had two young sons by his fourth wife, Obia (1), who died about two years ago. These boys were living with a childless matrilineal kinswoman of Obia's. They had gone to this kinswoman apparently because she had been a companion of their mother was herself childless and Okoi had at that time no obviously preferable way of arranging for their care since his other wives had several children of their own. Okoi was giving yams and presents to the woman. He did not anticipate their permanent adoption into the patriclan in which they are being brought up and the boys will probably claim his help when they are ready to marry and begin farming.

Okoi's household thus includes two adult men, Okoi and his grown up son, four wives, all of them women of middle age, and eleven minors of whom only six are children of both Okoi and the wife who has the care of them. It will however be seen from a review of the sequence of Okoi's marriages as shown diagramatically below that the household in 1935 was very different in composition from that of his early married life.

Table 13   Marriages and Births (including stillbirths) in the Household of Okoi   1905 - 1935

Husband
Okoi

m = birth of male child alive in 1935
m = "   "   "   "   dead
f = "   " female " alive "
f = "   "   "   "   dead
[ ] = child of previous husband with wife

y = wife previously unmarried
D = Divorcée

Okoi married his first wife, Akōwa (age set VII) just before the ceremonial establishment of his own age set in Ukpakapi ward in or about the year
1905, when he would have been about eighteen years of age. He had been betrothed to Akowa, who belonged to an age set immediately senior to his and
came from a patriclan of Biko-Biko ward, for two years before this and had
given the customary help to her father in his farm. After her first child
was born he built a woman's house for her in his father's compound, which
was now his own, and he began to farm for himself. But this child and several others died during the next four or five years in which Okoi, who was
a very capable farmer, built a harvest of over 100 sticks of yams,   as
large a harvest as a man with one wife could expect to achieve. A   second
wife would increase his harvest and perhaps be more successful in producing
a strong child. Marriage does not entail withdrawal of a young man   from
lovers' parties and Okoi had earlier associated at these with Okwō (age set
VIII) a girl of a different lineage in the same patriclan as that of   his
first wife and of an age set equivalent to his own. Okwō's father agreed
to their betrothal and Okwō became pregnant before marriage about four years
after his marriage to Akōwa. In seeking to marry her he complained to her
father, an elder of the clan, that his first wife who was from that clan had
failed to bear him a strong child. This was not strictly the father's concern, but Okoi claims to have secured some reduction of the marriage money
thereby, and he built a second woman's house for Okwō in his father's compound. Her first child, a girl, Edet (the only one of four now living) is
today married in Ukpakapi ward.

Akōwa, the first wife, eventually bore Okoi a son, Ūdūmō, his only a-
dult son today, but soon after this she quarrelled with her husband, return-
to her parents and subsequently married another man. Before this separation Okoi had married several other wives. He took a third wife Asibong (age
set VIII) of Ukpakapi ward a year after marrying Okwō. Asibong was betrothed to a man of Idjūm ward, who failed to make the marriage payment after her
likpokōt rite, and a few months <u>after</u> the birth of her child she agreed to
come to Okoi who offered a marriage payment. He brought Asibong to his compound after handing over the agreed marriage money, and thereby   acquired
the status of father of her child.

Before the next harvest Okoi married another young girl Obia (age set
IX) also from a patriclan in Ukpakapi ward to whom he had already been betrothed when he married Asibong. Obia (1) had six children in the   twelve
years before she died, but only two were alive in 1935, boys who were then
living with a childless matrilineal kinswoman of Obia in another patriclan
of Ukpakapi ward. Within three years of his marriage to Obia (1) Okoi married Abam (age set X) another young woman who soon after bore him her first
child.

For the next eight or nine years Okoi had five, and after the departure
of Akōwa four, wives and did not remarry. But in 1922 his second wife Okwō,

and two years later his fourth wife Obia (1) died. As he had an unusually large farm he needed the help of other women in their place and although he was over thirty-five years of age when Okwō died he became betrothed to a young unmarried girl Isū (age set XII) within a few months of Okwō's death and she came to his compound shortly before Obia died. A year or two later he brought to his compound as a wife an older woman Abima (age set X) who had deserted an earlier husband and for the next six or seven years Okoi again had an unusually large multiple household of four wives and over ten children until two of his wives deserted him.

Isū who got on badly with every one in the compound left him in 1933 taking two of her three young sons with her, and Asibong whose only surviving child, a youth on the verge of manhood, had just died, also deserted Okoi after a quarrel and went to live as a dependent of one of her matrilineal kinsmen soon after.

Okoi now had only two wives and to get all his yams cultivated more help was again essential. He brought to his compound in quick succession two women in their thirties who had left their former husbands, Edja (age set X) and Obia (2) (age set XII), and he is at present involved in a dispute over the marriage payments in connection with the last marriage.

The children of the wives who have died or have left Okoi have some of them gone to pass their childhood with their mothers or with relatives of their mothers, while others have been cared for by later wives. In the thirty years since Okoi first married thirty three children had been born to his household, apart from six still births; but in 1935 there were only eight of his own children in the household. One married daughter was living with her husband, two minors were living with their divorced mother, two others were living with a matrilineal kinswoman of their deceased mother, and twenty had died at various ages.

The Family. We are now in a position to consider the character and position in Yako social structure of the group to which the term family is generally applied, namely a group consisting of two parents and the dependent offspring.[1] It will have been clear from the foregoing exposition that the family in this sense constitutes the standard nucleus of the Yako

---

[1] While, as has often been pointed out (cf.Raglan, Man.31, 1931, 181) this use of the term is not etymotogically justified, it is convenient since it corresponds closely with the most usual meaning of the term in common speech by European peoples today while other meanings are covered by such terms as lineage and household. This group is sometimes distinguished from wider groups, formed by extension from it, as the 'simple' or 'elementary family'.

household. The significance of the fact that the Yakö, like many other peoples among whom the family group exists, have no distinctive term for it will become clear as the character of this group is considered. The Yakö family is a domestic association between a man and a woman which children born to them enter at birth but normally leave at marriage. The family originates in a publicly recognised partnership between man and wife for the begetting and rearing of children. It is, as has been seen, the prescribed unit of organisation of food supply and shelter dependent on a sexual division of labour, and provides for the custody and welfare of the children during their minority. The partnership involves specific and complementary rights and obligations on the part of both spouses, the observance and performance of which are sanctioned by the transfer of marriage money.

That the distinction between biological and sociological paternity is clearly recognised by the Yakö may be exemplified from the history of one of the marriages of an ina (matriclan priest) in Umor. When he was in his late middle age the priest offered betrothal gifts for a young woman whom he wished to marry, and with her parents consent he frequently spent the night with her in her mother's house. The girl became pregnant but early in the pregnancy quarrelled with the priest, one factor in the situation being apparently her age mates' disapproval of marriage with so old a man. The girl now declared that she would marry a youth her own age who had earlier joined her in night parties and had wished to be betrothed to her. To this, after some recrimination, the parents consented and a marriage payment was accordingly made by the young man at her likpököt.

Three or four years after the birth of her child and when she was living with her husband she sent a message secretly to the priest to say that she wished to come to him. When he consented to take her she left her husband and joined the priest who made a marriage payment to one of her matrilineal kinsmen from which the first husband was compensated. But the child, a boy whom the priest believes he begot during his betrothal to the woman stayed with the first husband, its socially recognised father. The priest has not only made no claim to the custody of the child but admitted that such a claim would not be recognised by public opinion, or by any authority such as the Village Head or the Native Court.

A family cannot endure longer than the partnership between the two parents while children born of the marriage, who belong to the family as dependents, leave it when adult to become one of the partners in the formation of another family. Thus a Yakö is born into one family, leaves it to establish another and expects to live to see the children born into that family depart from it to establish others. The family is therefore not a self-perpetuating group. It is on the contrary only an ephemeral and continually reconstituted organisation of certain domestic and par-

While the nucleus of the household is usually a family and the personnel of both may be identical the two are not necessarily or even generally coterminous. The household often includes other persons beside the father, the mother and their dependent children, while the family group itself may be disrupted completely by the divorce of the wife, or in part by the departure of young children to other households. Owing to the frequence of divorce and of the fostering of children the family group is in fact very often disrupted and many children are reared not in the families in which they were born but the households of step- or foster-parents.

It has often been asserted that kinship originates in the family which is to be regarded as the nuclear kinship unit from which other larger units are built up. This, among the Yakö, is assuredly not so;and it would not be difficult to show that the Yakö situation is one which is very general in societies in which unilineal kinship is a principle of organisation of considerable groups. The confusion underlying such notions results from failure to distinguish between the family as a group and the two distinct kinship relations established between a child and its father and mother respectively. Kinship relations admittedly derive from the begetting, bearing, and rearing of children and express institutionally the sentiments of parenthood and siblinghood. But the family itself is not a kinship group. From the point of view of kinship it divides into two distinct groups of which there is partial overlapping of personnel.These two groups are the father and the children who form a patrilineal unit group and the mother and the children who form a matrilineal unit group. These, not the family, are the basic units of the kinship system.

Among the Yakö there is rarely a lineal kinship relation between the father and the mother. Their relation is not conceived as one traced by chains of descent from a common ancestor. On the contrary marriage between members of a common patrilineal descent group is barred and between members of a common matrilineal descent group is not approved, while close relatives linked by a mixed chain of descent should not marry. Marriage does not make the man and wife kin either to each other or to the other's kinsfolk, and this is emphasised by the exclusion of one spouse from inheritance of any of the goods of the other.

While both father and mother claim kinship with the child, the principles of the kinship and the composition of the groups based thereon are entirely distinct. A child is by birth affiliated to the patrilineage and clan of its father and to the matrilineage and clan of its mother. A man is a patrilineal successor of his father and a matrilineal successor of his mother's brother. A woman is a matrilineal successor of her mother, but there is no transmission from her father. The Yakö family as a group has, in fact, no place in the kinship system. The disruption of a family

whether by divorce or by the death of one or both parents does not affect
the kinship affiliation of the children. Nor of itself does the fostering of children during minority by persons other than their parents.   It
has already been shown that a clear distinction should be made between the
fostering of children and adoption. The terms foster-father (or-mother)
and foster-son (or -daughter) are perhaps misleading when applied to the
Yakö situation for a foster-child does not when domiciled during minority
with a person or persons other than its original parents, thereby acquire
the formal status of a son or daughter of the fosterer. Intimacy and affection may be of the same order as in parentage but the socially recognised rights and obligations are not.

The status of sonhood to a foster-father can only be established when
the child has become adult and is founding with a spouse an independent
family group. If a man then receives from a fosterer with at least tacit
consent of his father or his father's patrilineal kin, the means of making a marriage payment and admission to land and domicile rights in
the fosterer's patriclan he ranks henceforth as the son of the fosterer
and no longer as the son of his father at birth. This transfer, which may
correctly be termed adoption, is, as has been shown earlier, essentially a
transfer of kinship affiliation with respect to patrilineal groups and
does not affect only the personal relations of the adopter and the son. It
is the disruption of one basic patrilineal kinship unit and the formation
of, or addition to, another; and with it is linked a corresponding change
in lineage and clan membership of the adopted man.

For a Yakö woman adoption does not exist and the rare occasions in
which a step-father receives the payment at her marriage are to be regarded as usurpations of the rights of the father or his patrilineal success-
or. In the same way an adoption can never follow from the rearing of a
child by a 'foster-mother' for no transfer of matrilineal affiliation is
recognised by the Yakö. A woman who fosters a child cannot in fact assume
with regard to it the formal relations and rights of a mother.

Foreign children introduced by purchase into Yakö households have
the status of sons and daughters of the head of the household or more
rarely of his wife but never of both. If the child was purchased by or on
behalf of a man it is recognised when adult as his son or daughter, but
it is also recognised as a matrilineal successor. The purchaser ranks in
fact as the mother's brother as well as the father of the child. A boy
will acquire land and residence rights through his purchaser in the latter's patriclan of which he is accepted as a member and the rule of patriclan exogamy will, among others, apply to him. But he will also rank
as a member of the purchaser's matrilineage and clan and as one of the
heirs to his moveable goods. To a girl who will rank as a daughter the
rule of kepün exogamy will similarly apply, but the father will also retain the entire payment at her marriage and she will be regarded as a mem-

ber of his matrilineage.

Married women, have also, sometimes with the help of a brother, acquired a purchased child whom they have reared in their households. Such a woman and her brother then have the rights and obligations of parentage with which the woman's husband is not concerned. A youth in such a case will be recognised at marriage as a member of the purchaser's brother's patriclan as well as one of his matrilineal heirs. The marriage payment will be handed directly to the brother and not to the woman's husband.

The customary attitude to the fostering of children and the transfer of rights involved in adoption serve to emphasise the fact that among the Yakö the family in not itself a kinship group but a domestic association by means of which the founding partners, the spouses, produce and rear children to whom they independently transmit distinct statuses and property rights. It is this separate transmission from each spouse and not the family as such which perpetuates the kinship structure from generation to generation.

Yakö marriage is an institution or social mode which regulates the mutual rights and obligations of men and women co-operating in the production of domestic supplies and the rearing of children. The transmission of moveable property and status in the matrilineal kinship system is independent of marriage; but as social recognition of fatherhood normally depends on a marital relation to the mother, marriage does determine patrilineal succession.

Nkɔ̃; 3, Fig 1.
Nkpani; 3, Fig 1.

Oil palm products; 4, 58, 65-6, 78, 103
Orthography; 4

Parental rights; 26,45,49,50,54-5
patriclan; 2,3,4,6,7,10,23,34,39,58,63,75,77,91-2,102,103,106-7
  - priest; 39,102
patrilineage; 6,10,34,53,71,91,102,103
plural wives; relations between -. 99-100
polygyny; 77,81,88-89
  - rates; 79,89
political organisation; 3
population; 3
  - changes; 96-8
post-marital residence; 37, 65, 99
pregnancy; 13, 20, 31, 37, 38, 42, 61
premarital pregnancy; 14

Radcliffe Brown, A.R.; 54
raphia palms; 65
reciprocity; 53
relative age at marriage; 83

Sampling; 2
seclusion of brides; 36-7
sex ratio; 81, 86, 89, 97
sexual behaviour; marital, 93
  - premarital, 13, 42
sociological paternity; 111, 112
statistical data; 2
step-father; 50
succession; matrilineal, 56, 70
  - patrilineal, 52, 56
suicide; 74

For Product Safety Concerns and Information please contact our EU
representative GPSR@taylorandfrancis.com
Taylor & Francis Verlag GmbH, Kaufingerstraße 24, 80331 München, Germany

www.ingramcontent.com/pod-product-compliance
Lightning Source LLC
Chambersburg PA
CBHW050718280326
41926CB00088B/3197